BRITISH
AIRCRAFT
OF WORLD
WAR II
WITH COLOUR
PHOTOGRAPHS

John Frayn Turner
Introduced by
Douglas Bader

BRITISH AIRCRAFT OF WORLD WAR II
WITH COLOUR PHOTOGRAPHS

Contents

Sidgwick & Jackson

Acknowledgements

I have been helped by various reference works in the
preparation of the statistical data for this book, but
I would like to mention particularly these three:

Aircraft of World War II by Kenneth Munson
Combat Aircraft of the World by John W. R. Taylor
Jane's All the World's Aircraft 1945–46

I am extremely grateful to the authors responsible
for these expert works. I must, however, accept
responsibility for any minor inconsistencies in the
specifications which are bound to occur in a book of
this nature.
I am also glad to acknowledge that the 'In Action'
section of the book includes material from various
official contemporary sources published by
H.M.S.O.—J. F. T.

Illustrations, pages 1-3
Page 1: Lancaster over Heinsberg during daylight
raid by R.A.F. Bomber Command on 16 November
1944
Previous page: Mosquito attacking and sinking
U-boat in the bitter Battle of the Atlantic

Designed by Paul Watkins
Picture research by Jonathan Moore

© Sidgwick & Jackson Ltd 1975
© John Frayn Turner 1975

ISBN 283 98180 6

Made and printed
by Morrison and Gibb Ltd, Edinburgh

Introduction by Douglas Bader

This is a splendid book. Its title belies the vast amount of information it contains. The aeroplanes flown by the Royal Air Force in World War II include a number of American types effectively used by all the Allied air forces, over land and sea, jungle and desert.

The generation which fought World War II on either side—German and British, American, and Japanese—is fascinated by the great interest shown by the present generation in that period of history, from 1939 to 1945.

This book is written with moderation by an expert in his subject—John Frayn Turner.

Information about the particular types of aircraft is supplemented by superb pictures in colour. But there is yet more. The author has included factual narratives of occasions when specific types were used effectively—or disastrously.

Anecdotes concerning some pilots whose names were household words thirty years ago add to the fullness of this book. In this context I cannot fail to mention a strange but true mental quirk of those who fly: that the recollection of a colleague in near-fatal distress in an aeroplane from which he subsequently escapes unhurt, is invariably the cause of tremendous mirth to his friends.

Many fine books have been written about the Hitler war. This is one of them.

The bookshelves of those who are interested in military aviation will be incomplete without it. I commend it wholeheartedly.

REFERENCE SECTION

A selection of specifications of the most important aeroplanes in service with the Royal Air Force during the Second World War. A number of aeroplanes of American manufacture, which were used extensively by the R.A.F., are also included. The letters 'NV' mean that the figures are 'not verifiable'—some specifications of the later wartime marks were not adequately checked and registered. The Victoria Cross symbol at the end of an aircraft entry indicates an account of how and when the Victoria Cross was won in that particular aircraft.

Albacore (Fairey)

Engine	One 1,065 h.p. Bristol Taurus II or 1,130 h.p. Taurus XII radial
Span	50 ft
Length	39 ft 9½ ins
Height	15 ft 3 ins
Weight empty	7,200 lb
Weight loaded	10,600 lb
Crew number	Two or three
Maximum speed	161 m.p.h. at 4,000 ft
Service ceiling	20,700 ft
Normal range	930 miles
Armament	Three .303 Vickers machine guns; six 250 lb bombs, or four 500 lb bombs, or one 1,610 lb (18 in.) torpedo

The Albacore was a torpedo-bomber flown from aircraft-carriers. It was meant originally to replace the Swordfish, but the latter in fact survived it. The Albacore design took the form of a biplane with wings foldable towards the tail so that it could be stored economically when aboard an aircraft-carrier. Among its features superior to the Swordfish were hydraulic flaps, an engine of greater power, an enclosed cockpit for a crew of two or three, and a slightly more modern look. The fuselage was metal monocoque in structure, with wings of fabric-covered metal. It could carry a single 1,610 lb torpedo, or half a dozen 250 lb bombs, or four 500 lb bombs. The Albacore joined Fleet Air Arm service in March 1940, initially flying from bases ashore on such tasks as patrols against enemy shipping and for mine laying operations. A year after entering service, it carried out its initial torpedo-firing action from a carrier, H.M.S. *Formidable*. This was in March 1941 at the Battle of Cape Matapan. From then on, the carrier-borne Albacores flew escort duties with Allied convoys in Baltic waters, as well as operating against submarines elsewhere. During duties from land bases in North Africa, Albacores were flown as spotters for artillery. In the weeks leading up to El Alamein, they were given the job of marking targets and troops by dropping no fewer than 12,000 flares. Fifteen squadrons of Albacores were flying at their 1942 heyday, but these fell to two by 1944. One of the Albacore's final missions was with the Royal Canadian Air Force in connection with the Normandy invasion. Altogether some eight hundred Albacores were built and enjoyed a varied and successful flying career from both land and sea bases.

Note: The Mark described in detail was the one most widely used in wartime.

Albemarle (Armstrong Whitworth)

Mk I

Engines	Two 1,590 h.p. Bristol Hercules XI radials
Span	77 ft
Length	59 ft 11 ins
Height	15 ft 7 ins
Weight loaded	22,600 lb (glider tug)
Weight loaded	36,500 lb (special transport)
Crew number	Four
Maximum speed	265 m.p.h. at 10,500 ft
Service ceiling	18,000 ft
Maximum range	1,300 miles
Armament	Four machine guns (bomber); two machine guns (glider tug and special transport)

The Albemarle was designed originally as a wood and steel bomber-reconnaissance aircraft, but by a quirk of circumstance it became a special transport, glider-tug and a paratroop-carrier. It had a 'tricycle' style of undercarriage, an innovation in the Royal Air Force. The Albemarle I was powered by two 1,590 h.p. Bristol Hercules XI engines. This first bomber-reconnaissance version reached the R.A.F. in January 1943. But subsequent variations served the purposes mentioned above instead. Some six hundred went into service altogether, transporting or tugging at various airborne landings. It took part as a glider-tug and a paratroop-carrier over Sicily on 10 July 1943; over France on 6 June 1944; and over Arnhem in September 1944. The Albemarle also carried mail and equipment to North Africa, Malta and Gibraltar.

Anson (Avro)

Mk I

Engine	Two 350 h.p. Armstrong Siddeley Cheetah IX radials
Span	56 ft 6 ins
Length	42 ft 3 ins
Height	13 ft 1 in.
Weight empty	5,375 lb
Weight loaded	8,000 lb
Crew number	Three
Maximum speed	188 m.p.h. at 7,000 ft
Service ceiling	19,000 ft
Normal range	660 miles
Armament	Two .303 machine guns; up to 360 lb of bombs

The Anson had the dual purpose of trainer aeroplane and also reconnaissance operational duty. Its design was developed from an Avro passenger transport of the early 1930s, with the original sole purpose of reconnaissance. A modern monoplane in configuration, it was powered by two 350 h.p. engines, while its armament comprised two .303 machine guns and 360 lb weight in bombs. The Anson began to enter Royal Air Force service in quantity from 1936 onwards, and at the outbreak of war began its reconnaissance role with R.A.F. Coastal Command. While it started to acquire a reputation in this field, it was also put into production for use as a trainer; 1,500 Ansons were built for the imaginative Commonwealth Air Training Plan. It carried out 'recce' duties for the first three years of the war, even claiming a Messerschmitt 109. The Anson II was constructed in Canada, using twin Jacobs engines instead of the Armstrong-Siddeley Cheetah. The Anson III was a version of the II made in Britain, while the IV switched from Jacobs to Wright Whirlwind engines. There then followed versions V and VI made in Canada to utilise plywood as much as possible, while further variations, up to XII, appeared in Britain. The figures quoted for Anson production, which went on years after the end of the war, were 8,138 in Britain and 2,882 in Canada. So the Anson serviced both the Royal Air Force and Royal Canadian Air Force, ending up perhaps better known as a trainer than for its original reconnaissance role: a typical twist in the life-story of an aeroplane.

Illustration in colour section

Baltimore (Martin)

Mk V

Engines	Two 1,700 h.p. Wright GR-2600-A5B5 Double Row Cyclone/Radials
Span	61 ft 4 ins
Length	48 ft 6 ins
Height	14 ft 2 ins
Weight loaded	22,622 lb
Crew number	Four
Maximum speed	320 m.p.h. at 15,000 ft
Service ceiling	25,000 ft
Normal range	980 miles
Armament	Ten machine guns: up to 2,000 lbs bombs

The Baltimore was a medium bomber acquired for the Royal Air Force. Although built in the United States, the aircraft never went into service with its country of origin. The Baltimore was a monoplane powered by two 1,600 h.p. Wright GR-2600-A5B engines. The considerable top-to-bottom depth of its body enabled its crew of four to enjoy good contact internally. Five versions of the Baltimore were flown for the R.A.F. The Baltimore I had a hand-operated Vickers K gun; II was armed with two such guns. In each case, these were additional to nine other guns: four guns in the wings, four other fixed-firing guns, and a single ventral. In the Baltimore III, four guns were housed in a dorsal turret; in the IV, a dorsal turret contained a pair of .50 guns; and the V changed to two 1,700 h.p. Wright GR-2600-A5B5 Double Row Cyclone radial engines. The Baltimore flew on bombing and reconnaissance roles in the Mediterranean and the Middle East from 1942-1945. Total production numbered 1,575.

Barracuda (Fairey)

Mk II

Engine	One 1,640 h.p. Rolls Royce Merlin 32 inline
Span	49 ft 2 ins
Length	39 ft 9 ins
Height	15 ft 1 in
Weight empty	9,350 lb
Weight loaded	13,916 lb
Crew number	Three
Maximum speed	228 m.p.h. at 1,750 ft
Service ceiling	16,600 ft
Normal range	684 miles
Armament	Two .303 Vickers 'K' machine guns; six 250 lb bombs, or four 450 lb depth charges, or one 1,620 lb torpedo

Barracuda: Comparison of Marks

		I		II		III		V	
Span	Ft in.	49	2	49	2	49	2	53	0
Length	Ft in.	39	9	39	9	39	9	41	1
Height	Ft in.	15	1	15	1	15	1	13	2
Weight	Lb	11,900		13,200		13,300		15,250	
Speed	m.p.h.	235		228		239		253	
at	Ft	11,000		1,750		1,750		10,000	
Ceiling	Ft	18,400		16,600		20,000		24,000	
Range	Miles	853		686		684		600	

There was no Barracuda IV built.

The triple-purpose Barracuda was a torpedo-bomber, a dive-bomber and also a reconnaissance aircraft – as well as being adapted for still other roles. Designed as a replacement for the older Albacore, this carrier-borne conception had to incorporate folding wings, which would flap to save space when stored aboard an aircraft-carrier. With its monoplane wings slung high across the fuselage and a similarly high brace to its tailplane, the Barracuda looked rather like the classic idea of the model-aircraft monoplane. Initial deliveries of this three-seater naval aeroplane started to reach the Fleet Air Arm in January 1943, half way through the war. After participating in the Allied assault on the Salerno beaches, that same year, the Barracuda reached what could be called its zenith with the Fleet Air Arm's role in the dashing, concentrated onslaught on the *Tirpitz* in April 1944. Barracudas took off from the decks of six British carriers and during the following months pressed home their airbone efforts against this German battleship. After the Barracuda I, powered by a Rolls Royce Merlin 30, came the II with the more powerful Merlin 32. The III combined torpedo-bomber and reconnaissance roles, complete with radar scanner in a radome beneath the fuselage. At various times, the Barracuda sported several of the following: a pair of machine guns, torpedo, mine, or four depth charges; rockets to assist take-off (R.A.T.O.) from shorter flight decks; radar and aerials; and perhaps most intriguing of all, special under-wing devices to house up to four Allied agents due for dropping into occupied Europe. Not a comfortable journey! There was no Barracuda IV built. The Barracuda V missed any operations due to the sudden end of the Far East war. It had a Griffon engine and was utilised as a trainer.

Battle (Fairey)

Engine	One 1,030 h.p. Rolls Royce Merlin I, II, III or IV
Span	54 ft
Length	52 ft 2 ins
Height	15 ft 6 ins
Weight loaded	10,792 lb
Crew number	Three
Maximum speed	241 m.p.h. at 13,000 ft
Service ceiling	23,500 ft
Normal range	1,050 miles
Armament	One .303 machine gun and one Vickers K gun and a 1,000 lb bomb load

The Battle was designed as a light bomber well before the war. A single Rolls Royce Merlin engine powered the aircraft. Over the course of the Battle's life, Merlin I, II, III and IV were all utilised, each having the same rating of 1,030 h.p. One of the principal features of the aircraft was its cantilevered, tapered wings set low into, and integrated with, its fuselage. The monoplane was all-metal in construction and although it marked a distinct advance on the pre-war biplanes it replaced, the Battle was soon regarded as obsolete in its turn. It was armed by a single .303 machine gun in one wing and a Vickers K gun mounted in the rear cockpit. It was a three-seater aeroplane. The most it could carry in bombs was 1,000 lb.

Despite the fact that its days were numbered when
war broke out, the Battle did, in fact, represent a foremost
part of the British Advance Air Striking Force across
the Channel in 1939. In the third week of the war, a
gunner operating from the rear of the Battle cockpit
chalked up the very first enemy aeroplane shot down
over France in the conflict. But the vulnerable Battle
sustained severe losses by 1940, and after the fall of
France its role was changed as soon as possible from
operational bombing to training and target-tug duties.
Despite a speed of 241 m.p.h., its light armament made
it prey to enemy fighters and its front-line life lasted
only for the first year of the war. A Battle flew for 2½
years with an electrically-operated contra-rotating
constant-speed airscrew – the first to be flight-tested in
Britain.

Only one man came back from a formation of
five Battle bombers that attacked a vital bridge
at Maastricht over the river Meuse on 12 May
1940. But two of the men who failed to survive this
suicide raid, Flying Officer D. Garland and Sergeant T.
Gray, were both awarded the V.C. posthumously – the
first V.C.s of the R.A.F. in the Second World War.
Garland led the attack and Gray was his observer. They
flew through a blizzard of shrapnel to carry out the order
to destroy the bridge at all costs – and the bridge was
duly blown. The cost was their lives and all the other
Battle aircrew, except the one man who survived.

Beaufighter (Bristol)

Mk X

Engines	Two 1,735 h.p. Bristol Hercules XVII radials
Span	57 ft 10 ins
Length	42 ft 6 ins
Height	15 ft 10 ins
Weight empty	15,600 lb
Weight loaded	25,400 lb
Crew number	Two
Maximum speed	303 m.p.h. at 1,300 ft
Service ceiling	15,000 ft
Normal range	1,470 miles (maximum)
Armament	Four 20 mm. Hispano cannon, one .303 Browning machine gun; one 1,650 lb or 2,127 lb torpedo; or 8 R.P. plus two 250 lb bombs

Beaufighter: Comparison of Marks

		IF	II	VIF	X TF
Span	Ft in.	57 10	57 10	57 10	57 10
Length	Ft in.	41 4	42 9	41 4	42 6
Height	Ft in.	15 10	15 10	15 10	15 10
Weight	Lbs	21,000	21,000	21,000	25,400
Speed	m.p.h.	321	301	333	303
at	Ft	15,800	20,200	15,600	1,300
Ceiling	Ft	26,500	NV	26,500	19,800
Range	Miles	1,170	NV	1,480	1,470

The Beaufighter was a home defence night-fighter, also used for long-range escort-fighter and ground-attack roles, as well as anti-shipping strike duties. Other roles were bomber, torpedo-carrier and rocket fighter. It represented some three-quarters of the airframe of the Beaufort, thus facilitating development and production. It was a two-seater, twin-engine design, whose considerable top speed of 303 m.p.h. and substantial armament combined to form a formidable adversary in its night-fighting and other roles. Its service started by September 1940 with Fighter Command, and by November, radar (airborne interception) equipment had been added for its night-fighter task. Armament comprised four 20 mm. cannon, and one .303 Browning machine gun. By the next spring, the Beaufighter entered another R.A.F. role, with Coastal Command. Soon the aircraft was flying not only over Britain, but also in the Middle East, India, Burma and the south-west Pacific area. The original U.S. night-fighter squadrons in Europe received their training in Beaufighters and flew into action with them over the Mediterranean in March 1944, during the Italian campaign. An array of versions of this versatile design began to emerge. The Beaufighter I had two Bristol Hercules III, X or XI engines; as a night-fighter the crew consisted of pilot and radio operator, who also acted as observer and cannon-loader. The II had Rolls Royce Merlin XX engines. The III experimental had Hercules III, X or XI engines. The IV was similar except for Merlin XX engines. The V had the same engines and was fitted with a four-gun turret behind the pilot's cockpit. The VI with Hercules VI or XVI engines had a Vickers K gun for the observer and was the first to carry rocket projectiles and torpedoes. The VII was never produced. VIII and IX were never allotted. X had Hercules XVII engines and was equipped as a long-range torpedo or rocket carrier. The XI had Hercules XVII engines and was a fighter for Coastal Command. The XII never went into production. The Mk 21 with Hercules XVIII engines was an Australian Beaufighter. Despite all its roles, it is remembered as being responsible for the halting of the enemy blitz on London in 1940–41.

Illustration in colour section

Beaufort (Bristol)

Mk I

Engines	Two 1,130 h.p. Bristol Taurus VI radials
Span	57 ft 10 ins
Length	44 ft 3 ins
Height	14 ft 3 ins
Weight empty	13,100 lb
Weight loaded	21,230 lb
Crew number	Four
Maximum speed	260 m.p.h.
Service ceiling	16,500 ft
Normal range	1,600 miles
Armament	Four .303 machine guns, up to 1,500 lb of bombs or mines, or one semi-external 1,605 lb torpedo

Beaufort: Comparison of Marks

		I	II
Span	Ft in.	57 10	57 10
Length	Ft in.	44 3	44 3
Height	Ft in.	14 3	14 3
Weight	Lb	21,230	22,500
Speed	m.p.h.	260	265
Ceiling	Ft	16,500	22,500
Range	Miles	1,600	1,450

The Beaufort was devised to meet the twin need for a land-based torpedo-bomber and also a reconnaissance-bomber. It was an all-metal, stressed-skin monoplane designed to be powered by two Perseus II or VI engines, replaced in production by Taurus VI, XII or XVI engines. There were four crew members. The Beaufort entered service at the end of 1939 and became recognised as the standard torpedo-bomber of R.A.F. Coastal Command for the following four years. Alternatively, it could, and did, carry bombs or mines. Armament consisted of two .303 machine guns capable of firing forward only from the nose of the fuselage, and a couple of machine guns in the dorsal turret. Later versions added to this armament by the incorporation of a remote-controlled machine gun with periscope sight, which could fire backwards from a 'blister' under the fuselage nose. For its role against enemy shipping, the Beaufort was installed with radar to detect vessels from the air. The Beaufort II was powered by two Pratt and Whitney Twin-Wasp radial engines driving constant-speed airscrews. Otherwise it remained virtually the same as the I. The aeroplanes served in many theatres of war, both naval and military: over the English Channel, Atlantic, North Sea, Western Desert and Mediterranean. One of their many highlights came in the desperate efforts to try and stop the *Scharnhorst*, *Gneisenau* and *Prinz Eugen* in their flight through the English Channel during February 1942. The Beaufighter eventually replaced the Beaufort as torpedo-bomber, but the aircraft continued to serve as a trainer. The Beaufort III, with two Rolls Royce Merlin XX engines, did not get beyond feasibility experiments. The Beaufort was also made overseas in Australia.

Illustration in colour section

Flying Officer K. Campbell was awarded the V.C. posthumously for his part in an attack by six Beaufort torpedo bombers on the *Gneisenau* at Brest on 6 April 1941. For various reasons it was eventually left to Campbell's Beaufort to make the vital attack. The aircraft had to fly through the most concentrated anti-aircraft barrage conceivable, from the flak ships below. The Beaufort flattened out of its dive only fifty feet above the water. They released their torpedo. Then the Beaufort was hit and crashed into the harbour. The torpedo struck the *Gneisenau* and eight months later its starboard propeller shaft was still under repair. Campbell and his crew were buried by the Germans in a grave of honour at Brest.

Blenheim (Bristol)

Mk IV

Engines	Two 920 h.p. Bristol Mercury XV radials
Span	56 ft 4 ins
Length	42 ft 9 ins
Height	12 ft 10 ins
Weight empty	9,800 lb
Weight loaded	14,400 lb
Crew number	Three
Maximum speed	266 m.p.h. at 11,800 ft
Service ceiling	31,500
Normal range	1,950 miles (maximum)
Armament	Five .303 Browning machine guns; 1,000 lb of bombs

Bristol Blenheim: Comparison of Marks

		I	IVF	VD
Span	Ft in.	56　4	56　4	56　1
Length	Ft in.	39　9	42　9	43　11
Height	Ft in.	12　10	12　10	12　10
Weight	Lb	12,250	14,400	17,000
Speed	m.p.h.	285	266	260
at	Ft	15,000	11,800	NA
Ceiling	Ft	32,000	31,500	31,000
Range	Miles	1,125	1,950	1,600

The Blenheim was a light/medium bomber remarkable for its speed. The maximum speed of the original Blenheim I was 285 m.p.h., considerably quicker than the pre-war fighters which were its contemporaries. The Blenheim was an all-metal monoplane of stressed-skin structure, powered by two Bristol Mercury radial engines. The three-crew bomber was defended by armaments comprising one .303 Browning machine gun and a Vickers K gun sited in a half-revolvable dorsal turret. As a bomber it could carry up to 1,000 lb of weapons. The Blenheim I was modified for service as a night-fighter, a testimony to its speed. An extra pack of four Browning machine guns were fitted beneath the bomb-bay position and an airborne interception radar was also added. The stub-nosed bomber helped defend against enemy night attacks following the Battle of Britain; it flew not only from Britain, but also in the Western Desert. After two non-productive versions, the Blenheim IV was built with more powerful engines – Bristol Mercury XV radials of 920 h.p., compared to the Mercury VIII at 840 h.p. Altogether 1,930 Blenheim IVs were produced, a greater number than the Is. Extra fuel tanks were incorporated

Below: Bombay with its unusually high-set wing. Powered by two Bristol Pegasus XXII engines

Below: Blenheims Mk IV in starboard echelon. They were useful light-medium bombers

Below: Blenheims Mk IV crewed by Free French air personnel serving in North Africa

in the wings and further refinements in this improved design included the protection of armour plate, a rear-firing machine gun in an under-nose 'blister', and twin machine guns in a 360-degree rotatable turret. A number of Blenheim IVs serving with Coastal Command had the earlier 'night-fighter' pack of four machine guns fitted under their fuselage. The last type was the Blenheim V, powered by two 950 h.p. Bristol Mercury XXX engines. During 1942, it saw operations in North Africa but it did not turn out to be either very successful or popular. Yet 940 were produced altogether and it was still in service a year or more later, not only in the Middle East but also against the Japanese. All five Royal Air Force Commands had Blenheims of one type or another, at one time or another – a tribute to this fast-flying aeroplane which was rather overtaken by the events during its long operational span from 1939–44.

Wing-Commander H. Edwards won the V.C. on 4 July 1941 as the leader of an attack by Blenheims on Bremen. Despite a balloon barrage and intense flak, they went in at fifty feet and actually cut telephone cables on their route. They hit their factory and port objectives, losing four bombers in the process. Edwards mustered the surviving Blenheims and led them home. When they landed, they discovered that every single surviving aircraft had been hit by flak or machine-gun.

On 9 December 1941, Squadron Leader A. Scarf won the V.C. in a Blenheim, though the award was not made till after the war. During a heavy attack by the Japanese on R.A.F. Butterworth, Malaya, two days after they had entered the war, every British aircraft was destroyed or damaged – except Scarf's Blenheim. Before the attack, the R.A.F. had been about to strike the enemy at Thailand. Scarf decided to undertake the mission alone.

He delivered his attack on Singora, but was hit and terribly wounded. He managed to fly his crew back towards his base and land. But he died in the operating theatre.

Wing-Commander H. Malcolm was awarded the V.C. posthumously not for one, but for three operations in seventeen days. On 17 November 1942, he carried out a low-level attack on Bizerta airfield without fighter escort and in broad daylight. On 28 November 1942, he repeated the raid, veering his leading Blenheim back again and again to attack the airfield with machine guns. On 4 December 1942, he was told to give close support to the First Army without fighter escort. Malcolm took ten Bristol Bisleys – the improved version of the original Blenheims – and reached the target. They delivered an attack from only two hundred feet against an enemy forward fighter aerodrome. Then all ten aircraft were destroyed one by one – Malcolm's being the last.

Bombay (Bristol)

Engines	Two 1,010 h.p. Bristol Pegasus XXII radials
Span	95 ft 9 ins
Length	69 ft 3 ins
Height	19 ft 6 ins
Weight loaded	20,000 lb
Crew number	Three/four
Maximum speed	192 m.p.h. at 6,500 ft
Service ceiling	25,000 ft
Normal range	2,230 miles
Armament	Two Vickers K machine guns and 2,000 lb of bombs

The Bombay was designed as a troop transport-bomber to lift either two dozen troops or 2,000 lb of weapons. The aeroplane had an unusually high-set monoplane wing, with Bristol Pegasus XXII radial engines in what have been called 'long-chord cowlings'. It was armed with a couple of Vickers K machine guns, one in each turret fitted at the fuselage ends. The number of crew could be three or four, depending on its role, the former when flown as a troop-carrier and the latter when intended for bombing duties. The Bombay had been designed long before the war and was considered comparatively out of date by 1939, when it finally reached the Royal Air Force. Nevertheless, some fifty aircraft flew in both the transport and night-bomber role. North Africa and the Mediterranean were its main spheres of operation, and its was over North Africa in the earlier stages of the war that the Bombay carried out bombing attacks by night.

17

Boston (Douglas)

III (DB-7B)

Engine	Two 1,600 h.p. Wright Double Cyclone radials
Span	61 ft 4 ins
Length	47 ft
Height	15 ft 10 ins
Weight empty	12,200 lb
Weight loaded	25,000 lb
Crew number	Four
Maximum speed	304 m.p.h. at 13,000 ft
Service ceiling	24,250 ft
Normal range	1,020 miles
Armament	Eight machine guns: up to 2,000 lbs of bombs

The Boston was an American light day-bomber as the name suggests. In the same way that it had taken over a French order for American Wildcats, the Royal Air Force also accepted the remainder of an order for the twin-engined DB-7 light bomber from France in 1940. The R.A.F. version of this was called the Boston I. These were employed as trainer aircraft to offer pilots and crew practical operating contact with nose-wheel landing gear. The Boston II then appeared and was adapted to night-flying in the fighter-intruder role. The titling got complicated at that stage as the aeroplane was re-christened the Havoc – presumably thought to be more in keeping with its aggressive aims. Four variants of the Havoc were developed, including one with a dozen machine guns in the transparent nose. The Boston III was the first DB-7 to be used by the R.A.F. as a

Left: Boston over Charleroi, France. Bombs are
falling from aircraft 'C' for Charlie

Below: The Botha with its two Perseus engines was a
torpedo bomber and a reconnaissance aircraft

day-bomber, the role for which it was originally designed.
This was followed by the Boston IV and V. One of the
Boston's attributes was its considerable speed as a
bomber, in excess of 300 m.p.h.

Botha (Blackburn)

Mk I

Engines	Two 880 h.p. Bristol Perseus X or 930 h.p. Perseus Xa radials
Span	59 ft
Length	51 ft $\frac{1}{2}$ in.
Height	14 ft $7\frac{1}{2}$ ins
Weight loaded	18,450 lb
Crew number	Four
Maximum speed	220 m.p.h. at 1,500 ft
Service ceiling	18,400 ft
Normal range	1,270 miles
Armament	Three .303 machine guns and one torpedo, or depth charges, or bombs

The Botha design had a twin purpose, like so many other
aircraft entering service about the start of the war and
soon afterwards. Its conception was as a torpedo-bomber
and a reconnaissance aeroplane for R.A.F. Coastal
Command. A four-crew monoplane powered by twin
Bristol Perseus X or Xa engines, it featured a
large-looking body. This was more than simple
appearance, for when the Botha first entered service in
June 1940, it was found to be under-powered for its
purposes. Its armament comprised two .303 machine guns
in a dorsal turret and a single forward-firing .303 machine

19

gun. Its intended offensive weapons were depth charges, a torpedo or bombs. Its career could not be classified as laurel-laden and in November 1940, the Botha was withdrawn from operations and downgraded to training purposes.

Catalina (Consolidated)

PBY-5A

Engine	Two 1,200 h.p. Pratt and Whitney R-1830-92 Twin Wasp radials
Span	104 ft
Length	65 ft 2 ins
Height	20 ft 2 ins
Weight empty	20,910 lb
Weight loaded	33,975 lb
Crew number	Eight
Maximum speed	179 m.p.h.
Service ceiling	14,700 ft
Normal range	2,350 miles
Armament	Five .50 machine guns

The Catalina was a famous flying-boat, designed for maritime patrol and reconnaissance and made in the United States primarily for the U.S. Navy. It derived from a civilian monoplane counterpart before the war and went into service with the U.S. Navy as early as 1936 under the designation of PBY-1. Two years later, the makers were allowed to export this design and the R.A.F. acquired one flying-boat in 1939. It was soon after this stage that the machine was christened Catalina by the Royal Air Force. By 1940 the variations had reached PBY-5A. The range reached over 2,000 miles and the power unit of the British Catalina comprised two 1,200 h.p. Pratt and Whitney R-1830-92 Twin Wasp radials. Defensive armament was five machine guns. Eventually no fewer than 650 Catalinas I and II joined the R.A.F. and the model was also produced in Canada for the R.C.A.F. Among the distinguishing features of the Catalina were its square-section wingtips, the 'blisters' in mid-fuselage and in a later version for the R.A.F., the Catalina VI, a specially tall fin. Both flying-boat and amphibious designs were built and used operationally from 1941 to 1945. The U.S. Navy naturally took most of these, but the Catalina proved valuable in R.A.F. Coastal Command. Carrying a crew of eight, it flew in its varied service over the Atlantic and many surrounding coastlines, as well as throughout the Pacific. And although classified for maritime-patrol and reconnaissance duties, between its U.S. Navy and R.A.F. years it also embraced service as a torpedo-bomber, convoy escort, rescue aeroplane, and materials transport. The Catalina was perhaps most famous for its remarkable range.

Two V.C.s were won by Coastal Command officers in Catalinas. They were Flight Lieutenant D. Hornell and Flying Officer J. Cruickshank. On 24 June 1944, Hornell and his Catalina were on anti-submarine patrols in northerly Atlantic waters. In an empty seascape, a U-boat appeared. A battle between giants ensued. The Catalina was hit mortally, but Hornell flew across the U-boat, releasing his depth charges and sinking the submarine. Then the burning starboard engine fell off the Catalina. Hornell somehow put it down on the waves. There followed 20 hours 35 minutes in a dinghy before they were rescued. One or two of the crew died before being picked up. Tragically, Hornell never regained consciousness. Five survived.

Flying Officer J. Cruickshank had the fantastic experience of being struck in seventy-two places by pieces of flak – and surviving these incredible injuries. With flak in his lungs and lower limbs, he flew his Catalina, attacked a U-boat – and sank it. Despite his wounds, he resumed command until he was sure his crew could get home safely.

Below: Catalina dropping smoke bombs. The aircraft
was powered by two Pratt and Whitney Twin Wasp
engines

Below: Dakota transport was used by both Britain and America. This C47B is dropping supplies to US troops near Corregidor

Right: Corsair X F4U-1 fighter prototype in original configuration. Below right: British Corsairs Mk II parked tightly aboard aircraft carrier off Norway

Corsair (Vought)

Vought F4U-1 (Corsair)

Engine	One 2,000 h.p. Pratt and Whitney R-2800-8 Double Wasp
Span	41 ft
Length	33 ft 4 ins
Height	16 ft 1 in.
Weight empty	14,000 lb
Crew number	One
Maximum speed	417 m.p.h. at 19,900 ft
Service ceiling	36,900 ft
Normal range	1,015 miles

This was the first American fighter to fly faster than 400 m.p.h. level. Both as a land and naval fighter, it was outstanding in the Second World War, and it was later produced for the British Fleet Air Arm under the nomenclature Corsair I, II, III and IV. These British versions were adapted to be housed on Royal Navy aircraft-carriers by clipping sixteen inches from the fighter's wings. The first record of British Corsairs going into operation was in the spring of 1944 aboard H.M.S. *Victorious* – some months before their American naval counterparts served at sea. A considerable consignment of Corsairs was also supplied to the Royal New Zealand Air Force. The latest American version was still in service with the U.S. Navy ten years after the war.

 On 9 August 1945, the war was nearly over. But Lieutenant R. Gray, a Canadian flying with the Fleet Air Arm, was leading his squadron of Corsairs off the flight deck of H.M.S. *Formidable* on a mission against the Japanese navy in the Bay of Onagawa Wan. He saw five or six vessels spreadeagled about the bay and dived down through anti-aircraft fire from shore as well as from ships. There was an outburst of fire as a shell struck the aircraft, ripping its fuselage. The firing intensified. Gray jerked the Corsair level again, one hundred feet from the destroyer straight ahead. Yet another shell was hurled into the fuselage. 'Bombs gone.' He had scored a direct hit. The destroyer exploded amidships and sank, as the Corsair dived into the blue Bay of Onagawa Wan.

Dakota (Douglas)

Mk I

Engines	Two 1,200 h.p. Pratt and Whitney R-1830-92 engines
Span	95 ft
Length	64 ft 6 ins
Height	16 ft 4 ins
Weight empty	16,865 lb
Weight loaded	25,200 lb
Crew number	Three
Maximum speed	230 m.p.h. at 8,500 ft
Service ceiling	23,200 ft
Normal range	2,125 miles (maximum)

The Dakota was the most extensively employed transport of the Second World War, under the designation of either C-47 Skytrain or Dakota. It was developed from the famous Douglas DC-3 twenty-eight seater commercial airliner. This low-wing cantilever monoplane was built in great quantities for the U.S. Army Air Forces, and no fewer than 10,000 had been delivered by the end of the war in Europe, the 10,000th actually coming off the production line on 5 May 1945. The Dakota I (American C-47) was used by the British as an all-purpose transport. It was really a cargo version of the DC-3 for large-scale military production, and it featured large loading doors, a reinforced floor, wooden seats, and glider-towing equipment. It was powered by two Pratt and Whitney R-1830-92 Twin Wasp engines. The Dakota III and IV had only minor amendments, the latter being evolved for the Indo-Chinese theatre of war. The C-53 was also

supplied to the R.A.F. as a Dakota and was the troop-carrying version of the C-47. It had no heavy cargo facilities – only a small door – and no reinforced floor. It could also serve as a supply-dropper and glider-tug.

The first member of R.A.F. Transport Command to be awarded the V.C. was Flight Lieutenant D. Lord. He was piloting a Dakota detailed to drop supplies at Arnhem on 19 September 1944. Although the starboard wing was set on fire and bound to collapse at any minute, Lord made a second run over the zone to drop remaining supplies. He then ordered his crew to abandon the Dakota, which was down to five hundred feet. He made no attempt himself to leave the aircraft and the starboard wing did in fact collapse, causing the aircraft to fall in flames. There was only one survivor.

Left: Defiant Mk I fighters of 264 Squadron R.A.F.
powered by Rolls-Royce Merlin XX engine. Below:
Defiant Mk II prototype with Rolls-Royce Merlin XX
engine

Defiant (Boulton Paul)

Mk II

Engine	One 1,260 h.p. Rolls Royce Merlin XX inline
Span	39 ft 4 ins
Length	35 ft 8 ins
Height	12 ft 2 ins
Weight empty	8,680 lb
Crew number	Two
Maximum speed	313 m.p.h. at 19,000 ft
Service ceiling	NV
Normal range	550 miles
Armament	Four .303 Browning machine guns

Defiant: Comparison of Marks

		I		II	
Span	Ft in.	39	4	39	4
Length	Ft in.	35	4	35	8
Height	Ft in.	12	2	12	2
Weight	Lb		8,600		8,680
Speed	m.p.h.		304		313
at	Ft		17,000		19,000
Ceiling	Ft		30,350		NV
Range	Miles		465		550

The Defiant was a fighter overshadowed by the Spitfire
and Hurricane. Its prototype flew first in August 1937,
and its unique claim was that it became the first fighter
in the world to incorporate a power-driven gun turret
instead of the conventional weapons which fired only
forwards. This called for a two-man crew. The Defiant
was a monoplane with low-slung wing and it had a

structure of all-metal stressed-skin. Its armament of four .303 Browing guns were all located in the turret to the rear of the pilot's cockpit. The Defiant I was powered by a single Rolls Royce Merlin III engine of 1,030 h.p. A month before the war broke out, the original production Defiant flew. It first operated as a daytime fighter on the historic date of 29 May 1940, over the beaches of Dunkirk. With its then maximum speed of 304 m.p.h. it went into successful action, claiming the destruction of 37 enemy aircraft without the loss of one Defiant. After its initial successes in May and June, the Defiant began to have its vulnerable under-belly attacked by the Germans, who were safe from the gun turret on top. Its losses soared and the Battle of Britain was left to the Spitfire and Hurricane. Fitted with airborne interception radar, the Defiant was then switched from day to night-fighter defence. The 1940–41 blitz on London proved the second highpoint in the history of the Defiant, when it brought down more enemy aeroplanes than other night-fighters of the time. The Defiant II was delivered in February 1941. The main change from the I was the more powerful Rolls Royce Merlin XX engine of 1,260 h.p. The Defiant II had a year of delivery life until January 1942, when the Defiant III appeared, actually intended as a target-tug. The Royal Navy also received a few Defiants for air-sea rescue work and other duties overseas. Production of Defiants totalled 1,060.

Firefly (Fairey)

F Mk I

Engine	One 1,730 h.p. Rolls Royce Griffon IIB, or 1,990 h.p. Griffon XII
Span	44 ft 6 ins
Length	37 ft 7 ins
Height	13 ft 7 ins
Weight empty	9,750 lb
Weight loaded	14,020 lb
Crew number	Two
Maximum speed	316 m.p.h. at 14,000 ft
Service ceiling	28,000 ft
Normal range	1,300 miles (maximum)
Armament	Four 20 mm. cannon; two 1,000 lb. bombs or eight 60 lb. RPs, optional

Firefly: Comparison of Marks

		I	IV
Span	Ft in.	44 6	41 2
Length	Ft in.	37 7	37 11
Height	Ft in.	13 7	14 4
Weight	Lb	14,020	14,200
Speed	m.p.h.	316	386
at	Ft	14,000	14,000
Ceiling	Ft	28,000	28,800
Range	Miles	1,300	1,070

The Firefly was the next naval fighter after the Fulmar, and from the same stable. Designed as a photo-reconnaissance fighter for aircraft-carrier operation with the Fleet Air Arm, the Firefly flew at 316 m.p.h., as against the 280 m.p.h. maximum of the Fulmar. In the intervening two years' development between the first flights of the Fulmar and Firefly, an advance was made by powering the latter with a 1,730 h.p. Rolls Royce Griffon IIB engine or a 1,990 h.p. Griffon XII. The most noticeable visual feature of the Firefly was probably the ellipse of its wing form; it also had an auxiliary lift from special flaps installed under the monoplane wing. The aeroplane was armed formidably with four 20 mm. cannon, and it could also carry a couple of 1,000 lb bombs or eight 60 lb rocket projectiles. The separate cockpit arrangements for pilot and navigator rather resembled the Fulmar layout. The Firefly II was a night-fighter version of the I, complete with special radar and other equipment, but this went into service only in small numbers. Two of the Firefly's major operational successes were first, the photo reconnaissance carried out on the *Tirpitz* before it was eventually sunk, and second, an attack on Sumatra oil refineries then in enemy hands. The Firefly was considered one of the finest Fleet Air Arm designs to take off from a flight deck during the war. The Firefly III did not go into production. The Firefly IV was one

of several post-war designs which pushed up the speed from 316 m.p.h. for the Firefly I to 386 m.p.h. for the Firefly IV.

Fulmar (Fairey)

Mk I

Engine	One 1,080 h.p. Rolls Royce Merlin VIII inline
Span	46 ft 4½ ins
Length	40 ft 3 ins
Height	14 ft
Weight empty	9,800 lb
Crew number	Two
Maximum speed	280 m.p.h.
Service ceiling	26,000 ft
Normal range	800 miles
Armament	Eight .303 Browning machine guns

The Fulmar was a two-crew fighter for the Fleet Air Arm conceived to operate from aircraft-carrier flight decks. The Fulmar I started its service in June 1940, less than six months after the prototype took to the air. Its most formidable feature was eight .303 Browning machine guns, the first fighter to join the Fleet Air Arm with this degree of armament. Designed for pilot and navigator, the monoplane had a sleek shape, the

navigator's cockpit being covered without protrusion above the rest of the fuselage form. The Fulmar I was powered by one 1,080 h.p. Rolls Royce Merlin VIII engine, while increased power was bestowed on the Fulmar II by the conversion to a 1,300 h.p. Rolls Royce Merlin XXX. The extra crew member and specialised equipment required for carrier operation helped to limit its top speed to 280 m.p.h. This hindered its success as a combat fighter. Despite such a handicap, however, the Fulmar did valuable duty, especially in the Mediterranean/Middle East zones. It was also flown extensively in other European areas and later in the Far East. Fighter,, convoy escort and reconnaissance tasks were among its many missions, and it ended up as a night-fighter. The Fulmar operated from 1940–45, enjoying distinct if limited successes with the six hundred and two aircraft produced altogether.

Gladiator (Gloster)

Mk I

Engine	One 830 h.p. Bristol Mercury IX radial
Span	32 ft 3 ins
Length	27 ft 5 ins
Height	11 ft 9 ins
Weight empty	3,217 lb
Weight loaded	4,594 lb
Crew number	One
Maximum speed	253 m.p.h. at 14,500 ft
Service ceiling	32,800 ft
Normal range	410 miles
Armament	Four .303 Browning machine guns

Gladiator: Comparison of Marks

		I		II		Sea Gladiator	
Span	Ft in.	32	3	32	3	32	3
Length	Ft in.	27	5	27	5	27	5
Height	Ft in.	11	9	11	7	11	7
Weight	Lb		4,594		4,864		5,020
Speed	m.p.h.		253		257		253
at	Ft		14,500		14,600		14,600
Ceiling	Ft		32,800		33,500		32,300
Range	Miles		NV		NV		NV

The Gladiator had two main claims to aeronautical fame. First, it was the very last biplane fighter to be flown in the Royal Air Force. Second, three Sea Gladiators, christened Faith, Hope and Charity, defended the island of Malta single-handed against the onslaught of the Italian air force for the latter part of June 1940, before further help arrived. The single-seater Gladiator was a development of the Gloster Gauntlet. It was an all-metal,

fabric-covered structure, agreed to have been not only the last, but also the best biplane fighter. Its main performance characteristics were a maximum speed of 253 m.p.h. and a service ceiling of 32,800 feet. The Gladiator I was powered by an 830 h.p. Bristol Mercury IXS radial engine and armed with four Browning .303 machine guns. These aeroplanes began their R.A.F. service as early as January 1937. The Gladiator II had a Mercury VIIIA engine. The Sea Gladiator was a II with either of the engines used on the Gladiator I and II. Its individual naval equipment included two features for use in conjunction with an aircraft-carrier – catapult points and an arrester hook, one to start it and the other to stop it. It also carried a dinghy in case of emergency landing over water. The Gladiator was in operational use from 1939–41. It distinguished itself not only in Malta; among the other war zones where the Gladiator flew and fought were Britain, Europe and Norway. Gladiator production totalled 648 aircraft, of which 216 were exported, and 98 Sea Gladiators. A memorable aeroplane reminiscent more of the First World War than the Second – and all the more remarkable because of that.

Halifax (Handley Page)

Mk III

Engine	Four 1,615 h.p. Bristol Hercules XVI radials
Span	104 ft 2 ins
Length	71 ft 7 ins
Height	20 ft 9 ins
Weight empty	38,240 lb
Weight loaded	65,000 lb
Crew number	Seven
Maximum speed	282 m.p.h. at 13,500 ft
Service ceiling	24,000 ft
Normal range	1,030 miles
Armament	Nine .303 Browning machine guns; up to 13,000 lb of bombs

Halifax : Comparison of Marks

		I		II		III	
Span	Ft in.	98	10	98	10	104	2
Length	Ft in.	70	1	70	1	71	7
Height	Ft in.	20	9	20	9	20	9
Weight	Lb	60,000		60,000		65,000	
Speed	m.p.h.		265		285		282
at	Ft		17,500		17,500		13,500
Ceiling	Ft	22,800		NV		24,000	
Range	Miles		1,860		NV		1,030

		V		VI		VII	
Span	Ft in.	104	2	104	2	104	2
Length	Ft in.	71	7	71	7	71	7
Height	Ft in.	20	9	20	9	20	9
Weight	Lb	60,000		68,000		65,000	
Speed	m.p.h.	NV		312		NV	
at	Ft	NV		22,000		NV	
Ceiling	Ft	NV		24,000		NV	
Range	Miles	NV		1,260		NV	

The Halifax was a heavy bomber powered originally by four 1,145 h.p. Rolls Royce Merlin X engines. When war broke out, the Halifax had not even made its maiden flight, yet by November 1940 it went into service with R.A.F. Bomber Command. The Stirling was the first of the four-engine heavy bombers in the Royal Air Force. Halifax followed soon afterwards. And from 1941–45 it became together with the Lancaster, one of the twin sources of bomber strength. Individual aircraft sorties numbered no fewer than 75,000, and it dropped over a quarter of a million tons of bombs. The Halifax called for a crew of seven and was designed for mass production to meet the offensive need. Its armament later reached nine .303 Browning machine guns and a 13,000 lb bomb load. After the Halifax I, the II had four 1,390 h.p. Merlin XX engines, while the III increased its power to four 1,615 h.p. Bristol Hercules XVI radials. The maximum speed was 282 m.p.h. Other variants of the III were a retractable tailwheel and extended wings. The IV was never put into production. The V featured a Dowty undercarriage. The VI took on still more power with its four 1,800 h.p. Bristol Hercules 100 engines. The VII had Hercules XVI engines and represented the last Halifax designed and made for bombing. The VIII was a transport aeroplane and the final Halifax IX was also a transport, but it was made after the war. A quantity of the Halifax II aircraft served with Coastal Command. Apart from its massive bombing role, the Halifax was flown for carrying paratroops and as a glider-tug. But of course its main job was as a prominent part of the four-year offensive by Bomber Command, culminating in late-April 1945 less than a fortnight before VE-Day. The total number of Halifax aircraft produced was 6,176.

Illustration in colour section

Hampden (Handley Page)

Mk I

Engines	Two 965 h.p. Bristol Pegasus XVIII radial
Span	69 ft 2 ins
Length	53 ft 7 ins
Height	14 ft 11 ins
Weight empty	11,580 lb
Weight loaded	18,756 lb
Crew number	Four
Maximum speed	265 m.p.h. at 15,500 ft
Service ceiling	22,700 ft
Maximum range	1,990 miles
Armament	Six .303 machine guns; up to 4,000 lb of bombs

The Hampden was a medium bomber which went into R.A.F. service a year before war broke out. Powered by two 965 h.p. Bristol Pegasus XVIII radial engines, the Hampden was at that time classified as a heavy, rather than medium, bomber. Its main visual features were the

tapering quality of the fuselage leading into a tail with twin fins and rudders. The four-man crew were located in the slim but deep section at the fore end of the body. The bomber could carry up to 4,000 lb of offensive weapons. When war started, however, its defensive armament was soon seen to be insufficient in the early daylight raids. The Hampden had four .303 machine guns originally, one with fixed firing and three with limited angles. These proved inadequate to defend it against enemy fighters, which inflicted considerable losses. To help remedy this deficiency, two of the three variable machine-gun locations had a pair each of Vickers K guns installed instead, bringing the total to six guns. The Hampden was in operational service with Bomber Command from 1939–42, being transferred in 1940 from day to night bombing. Among its many raids were participation in the very first attack on the German capital of Berlin, and the Cologne raid of 1,000 bombers. By the time the war had reached halfway, however, the Hampden was growing out of date as a bomber and flew for the final time with Bomber Command in September 1942. As so often happened, this aeroplane of only limited success in one sphere, then went into a role more appropriate to its design, and with greater success. The Hampden became a torpedo-bomber and mine-layer with R.A.F. Coastal Command, where its qualities suited the weapons and conditions. It continued on these duties until 1944, having served for five of the six years of the war. An early variant of the Hampden was the Hereford, virtually the same aeroplane but powered by two 955 h.p. Napier Dagger VIII engines. These were restricted to a training role.

Flight Lieutenant R. Learoyd was awarded the V.C. for his part in an attack by eleven Hampdens against the old aqueduct on the Dortmund-Ems canal on 12 August 1940. The purpose was to try and paralyse transport on this waterway. The Hampden was repeatedly hit and large chunks of the main planes torn away as they descended to 150 feet. But together with the other bombers, they accomplished their mission of destroying the aqueduct. The Hampden's hydraulic system was out of action, as well as having sustained much other damage, so that when Learoyd finally got it back to Britain, he had to fly around for a further 2½ hours until dawn before attempting to land.

The youngest R.A.F. man ever to win the V.C. was Sergeant J. Hannah, also in a Hampden, on 15 September 1940. This 18-year-old was over Holland when the bomber was hit and set on fire. Badly burned and almost blinded by heat, Hannah fought the fire in the bomb compartment while his pilot struggled for home. He saved their lives and also the Hampden.

Harvard (North American)

Mk II B

Engine	One 550 h.p. Pratt and Whitney Wasp radial
Span	42 ft 0¼ in.
Length	29 ft
Height	11 ft 8½ ins
Weight empty	4,158 lb
Weight loaded	5,250 lb
Crew number	Two
Maximum speed	205 m.p.h. at 5,000 ft
Service ceiling	21,500 ft
Normal range	750 miles
Armament	None

The Harvard was a two-seater advanced-pilot trainer. This low-wing monoplane was powered by one 550 h.p. Pratt and Whitney Wasp radial engine. Seating was in tandem under a single enclosure, but with individually operated sliding panels for each person. As normal with trainers, dual installations were fitted for both flight and power controls. It had the comfortably low landing speed of 67 m.p.h. Manufactured in America, the square-wing Royal Canadian Air Force Harvards were much in evidence in the Canadian skies as a vital trainer in the British Commonwealth Air Training Plan. The total number of pilots graduating from this scheme reached a staggering 131,553. The Harvard was also familiar on Allied airfields in various theatres of war, with the American as well as British Commonwealth air forces.

On the night of 30 March 1944, ninety-six bombers were reported missing from the night's raid on Germany. It was one of the heaviest Allied losses of the war. Pilot Officer C. Barton was captain of a Halifax detailed to attack Nuremberg. A Junkers 88 swooped on the bomber as it was some seventy miles short of the night's main target. An Me 210 joined in as well. The inter-com system was destroyed, an engine damaged, and the bomber's machine guns put out of action. Through a mix-up in signals, the navigator, air bomber and wireless operator left the aircraft by parachute. Barton could not communicate with the rest of his crew. But he reached the target and released the bombs himself. Then the propeller of the damaged engine flew off. Two of the petrol tanks were leaking. Somehow he got his Halifax back across the English Coast – a 4½-hour flight over heavily defended territory. The port engines stopped, but Barton managed to crash-land the bomber. The three members of the crew survived, as did the other three who baled out by mistake over Germany; but Barton died.

Illustration in colour section

Hind (Hawker)

Engine	One 640 h.p. Rolls Royce Kestrel V
Span	37 ft 3 ins
Length	29 ft 7 ins
Height	10 ft 7 ins
Weight empty	5,298 lb
Weight loaded	NV
Crew number	Two
Maximum speed	186 m.p.h. at 16,400 ft
Service ceiling	26,400 ft
Normal range	430 miles (maximum)
Armament	One Vickers gun and one Lewis gun; up to 500 lb of bombs

The Hind was the final biplane design of light bomber to enter Royal Air Force service. It carried a crew of two and was powered by a single 640 h.p. Rolls Royce Kestrel V engine. The total weight of bombs that could be carried was 500 lb; its defensive armament was as light as its bomb load and consisted of a Vickers machine gun and a Lewis gun, fired from the bomber's rear cockpit by the second crew member. Two years before war broke out, the Hind was still the most advanced R.A.F. light bomber, but it was rapidly superseded by the Blenheim and the Battle. Some of the 528 Hinds which joined the Royal Air Force were then adapted for use as training aircraft. The Hind served with the Auxiliary Air Force until just before the War.

Hudson (Lockheed)

Mk III (A-29)

Engines	Two 1,200 h.p. Wright R-1820-87 Cyclone radials
Span	65 ft 6 ins
Length	44 ft 4 ins
Height	11 ft 11 ins
Weight empty	12,825 lb
Weight loaded	20,500 lb
Crew number	Five
Maximum speed	253 m.p.h. at 15,000 ft
Service ceiling	26,500 ft
Maximum range	1,550 miles
Armament	Five machine guns; up to 1,600 lb of bombs

The Hudson was a maritime-reconnaissance bomber. It was designed and made in the U.S., having been adapted from a pre-war American airliner. The Hudson went into service with R.A.F. Coastal Command just before the outbreak of war. Exactly five weeks after war started, a Hudson was credited with the destruction of the first enemy aircraft by the Royal Air Force. One of the visual features of the Hudson was the row of portholes along its fuselage, derived from its airliner origins. The Hudson I had two 1,100 h.p. Wright engines. The Hudson II was powered by two 1,200 h.p. Wright R-1820-87 Cyclone radial engines. It carried a crew of five, flew at a top speed of 253 m.p.h., and possessed the valuable maximum range of 1,550 miles. Its bomb load could tally 1,600 lb – one-tenth that of a Lancaster! Its long reconnaissance range helped it to trace the Altmark in 1940. Slight variations of the Hudson continued to be made in America and delivered to the R.A.F. Hudsons flew

offensive reconnaissance sorties from 1939–43, when, incidentally, one destroyed a German submarine by rocket armament. After that time they also flew in valuable transport and rescue roles.
Illustration in colour section

Hurricane (Hawker)

Mk IIB

Engine	One 1,280 h.p. Rolls Royce Merlin XX inline
Span	40 ft
Length	32 ft
Height	13 ft 1 in.
Weight empty	5,640 lb
Weight loaded	8,250 lb
Crew number	One
Maximum speed	339 m.p.h.
Service ceiling	36,000 ft
Normal range	470 miles
Armament	Twelve .303 Browning machine guns.

Hurricane: Comparison of Marks

		I		IIA		IIB	
Span	Ft in.	40	0	40	0	40	0
Length	Ft in.	31	5	32	0	32	0
Height	Ft in.	13	1	13	1	13	1
Weight	Lb	6,600		8,050		8,250	
Speed	m.p.h.	324		342		339	
at	Ft	NV		NV		NV	
Ceiling	Ft	34,200		36,300		36,000	
Range	Miles	425		470		470	

		IIC		IID		IV	
Span	Ft in.	40	0	40	0	40	0
Length	Ft in.	32	0	32	0	32	0
Height	Ft in.	13	1	13	1	13	1
Weight	Lb	8,100		7,850		8,450	
Speed	m.p.h.	336		322		330	
at	Ft	NV		NV		NV	
Ceiling	Ft	35,600		32,100		32,600	
Range	Miles	460		420		430	

The Hurricane was a wonderful British aircraft – and the very first monoplane fighter ever to enter Royal Air Force service. It inscribed its immortality, along with the Spitfire, in the Battle of Britain. The Hurricane served throughout the entire war and was flown on no fewer than seventeen different battlefronts: Britain, France,

Norway, North Africa, Sicily, Italy, Middle East, Far East, Russia, Adriatic, Atlantic, Mediterranean and Northern Convoys – to quote only the most memorable. It was a fighter, fighter-bomber, rocket-projectile fighter, and tank-buster – apart from the Sea Hurricane version dealt with separately. The Hurricane was designed by Sydney Camm and the prototype made its maiden flight on 6 November 1935. It was put into production in 1936, six hundred being ordered initially. The production Hurricane flew first in October 1937, and it reached squadron service in December 1937. This marked the start of over 14,000 Hurricanes being built between 1937 and 1944. The Hurricane I had a Rolls Royce Merlin II engine of 1,030 h.p., and it was armed with the weaponry of eight Browning machine guns – four in each wing. In the Battle of Britain, the Hurricane was flown by about six out of every ten squadrons, and it accounted for more enemy aircraft destroyed than any other type of British aircraft. In the first year or so of the war, until the end of the Battle of Britain, the Hurricane shot down more than 1,500 of the enemy in confirmed successes. This figure represented nearly half of the total of all enemy aircraft which the Royal Air Force destroyed during that period.

By the time of the Battle of Britain, the Hurricane II was already in production. This had an even deadlier armoury of twelve machine guns (IIB), or four 20 mm. cannon (IIC). The engine was now the 1,280 h.p. Merlin XX. The IIB and IIC could also have racks fitted to take two 250 lb or 500 lb bombs – or two 44 or 90 gallon drop fuel tanks. These fighter-bombers were unofficially christened Hurribombers and flew into the offensive over occupied France in November 1941. The maximum speed of the IIB fighter was 339 m.p.h. The Hurricane, of course, originally represented the first R.A.F. fighter to exceed the magic speed of 300 m.p.h. By about 1942, the Hurricane changed its basic role from interceptor-fighter to ground attack with still more powerful armament. Rocket projectiles yielded tremendous extra power, while 40 mm. cannon doubled the calibre of their predecessors. This cannon-carrying Hurricane IID had a maximum speed of 322 m.p.h., but the armoury did great damage to the German tanks in North Africa. The era of the IID began in 1942. Then in 1943 came the Hurricane IV with a 1,620 h.p. Merlin 24 or 27 engine. This could permutate any of the following alternative armaments and loads: two 40 mm. cannon and two .303 machine guns; eight rocket projectiles and two .303 machine guns; two 250 lb or 500 lb bombs and two .303 machine guns; two 44 or 90 gallon drop tanks and two .303 machine guns. Its top speed was 330 m.p.h. The Hurricane V had a Merlin

27 or 32 engine, but only two were ever built. The Hurricane X with a Packard Merlin 28 engine was built in Canada; so were the Hurricanes XII and XIIA, powered by a Packard Merlin 29 engine.
Illustration in colour section

Flight Lieutenant J. Nicolson was the only fighter pilot to win the V.C. in the Battle of Britain. Flying his Hurricane on 16 August 190, he intercepted the enemy over the Southampton area. During a combat with a Messerschmitt, his Hurricane was hit by four cannon shells. One pierced the cockpit, injuring one of his eyes; another hurt his foot; the remaining two damaged the engine and set fire to the gravity tank. Petrol poured out and seeped into the cockpit as flames started to spread. Just as Nicolson was about to struggle out of the cockpit, he saw another Messerschmitt. He slid back into the cockpit, up to his waist in flames. He fired at the enemy, destroyed it, and then somehow baled out of the blazing Hurricane. Nicolson survived the burns, but died during 1945 in a Liberator crash.

Lancaster (Avro)

Mk III

Engines	Four 1,460 h.p. Rolls Royce Merlin XX or XXII, or 1,640 h.p. Merlin XXIV
Span	102 ft
Length	69 ft 6 ins
Height	20 ft 6 ins
Weight empty	37,000 lb
Weight loaded	68,000 lb
Crew number	Seven
Maximum speed	287 m.p.h.
Service ceiling	19,000 ft
Maximum range	2,530 miles
Armament	Ten .303 Browning machine guns; up to 14,000 lb of bombs normally

Lancaster: Comparison of Marks

		I	II	III	VI	VII
Span	Ft in.	102 0	102 0	102 0	102 0	102 0
Length	Ft in.	69 6	69 6	69 6	69 6	70 5
Height	Ft in.	20 6	20 6	20 6	20 6	20 6
Weight	Lb	65,000	63,000	68,000	NV	72,000
Speed	m.p.h.	287	270	287	NV	275
at	Ft	NV	NV	NV	NV	NV
Ceiling	Ft	19,000	19,000	19,000	NV	NV
Range	Miles	2,530	2,530	2,530	3,800	NV

The Lancaster was the most illustrious heavy bomber to fly with the Royal Air Force in the Second World War. It was developed from the unfortunate Manchester twin-engine medium bomber. The Lancaster prototype with four Rolls Royce Merlin X 1,145 h.p. engines was actually referred to at first as the Manchester III. Then the Lancaster I made its entrance very early in 1942, powered by four 1,280 h.p. Rolls Royce Merlin XX engines and armed with ten .303 Browning machine guns. The maximum bomb load was the then phenomenal figure of 14,000 lb. The Lancaster began its three-year career as a night-bomber, dropping altogether over 600,000 tons. The bomber could carry and accommodate single bombs weighing 4,000 lb, 8,000 lb and later 12,000 lb. The most memorable action by Lancasters was of course the Dam Busters raid on the Mohne and Eder dams in May 1943. Although the normal bomb load was 14,000 lb, it could in fact be increased to 18,000 lb with no modification being necessary. With appropriate adaptation, the bomb-bay of the Lancaster could take not only the 12,000 lb bomb, but also the great Grand Slam bomb weighing 22,000 lb. The Lancaster was the only aircraft in the war which bore bombs of such weight. After the Lancaster I came the II, powered by four 1,650 h.p. Bristol Hercules VI air-cooled radial engines. This was followed by the III, similar to the I except that it was fitted with four Packard-built Merlin engines: 28, 38 or 224. The Lancaster IV and V went into service as the Lincoln I and II – scaled-up versions of the Lanc – while the VI introduced electronic jamming equipment. The VII had a dorsal turret placed further forward than in previous designs. The Lancaster X was the designation for the III when built in Canada. The last Lancaster exploit to go down in history was the sinking of the *Tirpitz*, but its fame rests on its night-bombing, particularly the attack on the dams.

Illustration in colour section

Many Lancaster aircrew were awarded the V.C. The first was Squadron Leader J. Nettleton, who led the dozen Lancasters in the daring daylight raid against the U-boat engine factory at Augsburg on 17 April 1942. Nettleton's aircraft was riddled with fire but he 'brought it back alive' – the only one of his flight of six to survive. Seven out of the twelve Lancasters were lost.

Flight Lieutenant W. Newton was the only member of the Royal Australian Air Force to be awarded the V.C. He carried out 52 sorties from May 1942 to March 1943, and 16 March 1943, Newton flew the first of two particularly hazardous missions in New Guinea. On 17 March he was lost after bringing his blazing bomber down on the water to enable two of his crew to escape. Newton was taken prisoner and killed by the Japanese.

The next Lancaster V.C. was Wing-Commander G. Gibson, awarded for the immortal Dam Busters raid on the night of 16–17 May 1943. Nineteen Lancasters took off, eight failed to return. Yet without Gibson's heroism, both at Mohne and Eder, in drawing enemy fire on his own bomber, the losses would have been heavier.

Flight Lieutenant W. Reid was awarded the V.C. for his great bravery on 3 November 1943: 'Wounded in two attacks, without oxygen, suffering severely from cold, his navigator dead, his wireless operator fatally injured, his aircraft crippled and defenceless, Reid showed superb courage and leadership in penetrating into enemy territory to attack one of the most strongly defended targets in Germany.' Reid brought the bomber back, despite a head wound.

Warrant Officer N. Jackson became the first flight engineer to win the V.C. This was the last sortie of his second tour. The date was 26 April 1944 and the target Schweinfurt. The Lanc dropped its bombs and was climbing out of the inferno of the target area when an enemy fighter hit it time after time. Fire broke out on the starboard wing. Jackson sustained wounds from shell splinters, but said he could deal with the fire. He started to climb out of the cockpit along the top of the fuselage to the wing in the fiery black night. But his parachute pack opened and the whole canopy streamed into the cockpit. In intense cold, he got to the wing but lost his fire extinguisher. He got back into the Lanc but by now the captain had ordered 'Abandon ship'. Four got away safely, two died. Jackson was severely charred and his parachute badly burned but he managed to bale out and survive as a prisoner of war.

Pilot Officer A. Mynarski was awarded the V.C. posthumously. He was the mid-upper gunner of a Lancaster detailed to attack a special target at Cambrai, in France, on 12 June 1944. Both port engines failed at once due to enemy fighter attack. Fire broke out and the captain ordered 'Abandon ship'. But Mynarski stayed to try and get through to free the trapped rear gunner – although he was himself in flames. He could not do so. He turned towards the gunner and although in agony, saluted him. Then Mynarski jumped out. French people on the ground watched his burning descent, as if a human torch were tracing a message. Mynarski died, yet by a quirk of fate, the rear gunner survived the crash landing.

Three of the last six V.C.s of the air were members of the famous Pathfinder force of R.A.F. Bomber Command. On 4 August 1944, Squadron Leader I.

Bazalgette was in command of a Lancaster detailed to mark a vital rocket and bomb site. The Lanc's starboard engines were both put out of action and fire swept the fuselage. But Bazalgette marked the target for the following bombers. Then the port inner engine failed and the whole starboard mainplane melted into flames. Some of the crew baled out to safety. But the bomb-aimer and mid-upper gunner were trapped, so Bazalgette stayed at the controls and made a crash landing. The Lancaster jerked to a halt – and exploded. All three men died.

Squadron Leader R. Palmer was on his 111th mission on 23 December 1944, when he led Lancasters to attack marshalling yards at Cologne in daylight. Palmer's Lanc was the first Pathfinder. He lost two engines before reaching the target, but did not diverge from his course. His bombs hit the target bang in the middle, and the Lancaster was last seen spiralling to earth in flames.

Flight Sergeant G. Thompson was awarded the V.C. posthumously for a daylight raid on 1 January 1945 against the Dortmund-Ems canal. Despite being badly burned, he saved two gunners trapped by flames in an inferno of a bomber. Then he crawled back to his captain to report the situation. The pilot crash-landed the crippled Lanc near a Dutch village. One of the two gunners survived, but Thompson died later.

The last Lancaster V.C. awarded posthumously went to Captain E. Swales of the South African Air Force. He was master-bomber of a force that attacked Pforzheim on 23 February 1945. The aircraft was badly damaged during the mission and lost height steadily on the return route. They were by now over friendly territory, so Swales ordered his crew to bale out. Hardly had the last one jumped, than the aircraft plunged to earth. Swales was found dead at the controls.

Liberator (Consolidated)

Mk VI

Engines	Four 1,200 h.p. Pratt and Whitney Wasp R-1830-65
Span	110 ft
Length	67 ft 2 ins
Height	18 ft
Weight empty	36,500 lb
Weight loaded	65,000 lb
Crew number	Eight-ten
Maximum speed	290 m.p.h. at 25,000 ft
Service ceiling	28,000 ft
Normal range	2,100 miles
Armament	Ten .50 machine guns; 8,800 lb of bombs

The Liberator was the British name for an American bomber, transport and reconnaissance aircraft which was in international service from 1941–45. It went into production during autumn 1940 and was not withdrawn until after VE-Day. Total output was in the region of 19,000. The very first Liberators to be made were allocated to Britain, but they did not prove to be qualified for service as bombers. Then the Liberator I reached R.A.F. Coastal Command. It was powered by four Pratt and Whitney R-1830-33 engines. Its American armament comprised six .50 and two .30 flexible guns, while the R.A.F. version had five .50 machine guns. and a battery of fixed guns beneath the fuselage. The purpose of the Coastal Command aircraft was to bridge the gap in the Atlantic between Britain and the U.S.A. not previously covered by patrol bombers. The Liberator II had R-1830-S3C4G engines. It carried a crew of ten and

became bomber and transport with Coastal Command. The Liberator III joined the same command and was the first model to take two 4,000 lb bombs. The III was also flown for general long-range reconnaissance. It was adequately defended and could carry bombs or depth charges to a weight of 8,800 lb. The R.A.F. had 260 of this mark. Its U.S. designation was B.24D. Quantities of the Liberator IV flew with Bomber Command as well as Coastal Command. Finally the Liberator VI had improved armament and could carry 8,800 lb of bombs or depth charges. There was also a reconnaissance version. The U.S. type bore the mark B-24H/J. The Liberator flew with U.S. Flying Fortresses over Europe and also in the Mediterranean areas. However its range made it specially suited to the Far East theatre, where the distances to be flown were greater. The Liberator proved to be a valuable and versatile aircraft, flown in virtually every role. American and British versions dropped a total of over 600,000 tons of bombs on the enemy.

Flying Officer L. Trigg was the first airman to be awarded the V.C. while on operations against a U-boat. It was bestowed posthumously as a result of evidence originating entirely form the enemy. On 11 August 1943, Trigg was the captain of a Liberator bomber on patrol when he spotted a U-boat. His bombs hit the enemy, but shells from their new large-bore guns also hit the Liberator repeatedly. But he continued the attack, skimming over the submarine at less than fifty feet. He dropped his last bombs and saw them doom the U-boat, before limping clear and then diving into the sea. Some of the Germans subsequently rescued by the R.A.F. were generous in their praise of the Liberator crew. They were 'expendable' in the Battle of the Atlantic, but without them and other such crews it could never have been won.

Lysander (Westland)

Mk I

Engine	One 890 h.p. Bristol Mercury XII radial	
Span	50 ft	
Length	30 ft 6 ins	
Height	14 ft 6 ins	
Weight empty	4,065 lb	
Weight loaded	5,920 lb	
Crew number	Two	
Maximum speed	219 m.p.h. at 10,000 ft	
Service ceiling	26,000 ft	
Normal range	500 miles	

Armament	Three .303 machine guns; 16 × 20 lb or 4 × 120 lb or 2 × 250 lb bombs

Lysander: Comparison of Marks

		I	IIISAS
Span	Ft in.	50 0	50 0
Length	Ft in.	30 6	30 6
Height	Ft in.	14 6	14 6
Weight	Lb	5,920	6,318
Speed	m.p.h.	219	207
at	Ft	10,000	10,000
Ceiling	Ft	26,000	21,500
Range	Miles	600	NV (endurance 8 hours)

Lysander was a unique aeroplane designed for R.A.F. Army co-operation – but destined to go down into aviation history for its part in dropping agents into Europe. The Lysander had a crew of two and was powered by a single 890 h.p. Bristol Mercury XII radial engine. It had the distinctive appearance of a bird, with its ultra-wide undercarriage feet and high wings which looked as if they were flapping. When on reconnaissance, its engine also emitted a distinctive drone. The Lysander went into R.A.F. service in 1938. During 1939–40 it was flown over North Africa as well as France, before the fall of that country. The Lysander II was powered by a 905 h.p. Bristol Perseus XII engine, while the III had a Bristol Mercury XX or XXX engine of 870 h.p. Armed with three .303 machine guns and small bombs, the Lysander also indulged in variegated air duties, including day ground attack; fighting by night; and target-towing. But, fitted with an extra fuel tank, the Lysander III is best remembered for its role in transporting and dropping Allied agents onto the Continent, to be met by the Resistance. The rather graceless, yet valuable Lysander served operationally from 1934–44.

Manchester (Avro)

Mk I

Engine	Two 1,760 h.p. Rolls Royce Vulture inlines
Span	90 ft 1 in.
Length	70 ft
Height	91 ft 6 ins
Weight empty	50,000 lb
Crew number	Seven
Maximum speed	265 m.p.h. at 17,000 ft
Service ceiling	19,200 ft
Maximum range	1,200 miles
Armament	Eight .303 machine guns; up to 10,350 lb of bombs

The Manchester was a medium bomber based on two 1,760 h.p. Rolls Royce Vulture engines. This unhappy aircraft could have had a very different career if its engines had not proved inadequate on two counts: they did not generate sufficient power for its bulk, nor could they be relied upon to provide faultless running service. These flaws combined to cause losses. The Manchester possessed perfectly sound aeronautical characteristics. It could fly up to 265 m.p.h. at 17,000 feet; could carry over 10,000 lb of bombs; was fully armed; and could claim a range of 1,200 miles. The bomber first saw service in November 1940. A couple of hundred were operational altogether, before being retired prematurely twenty months later. It called for a crew of seven, who criticised it with good reason for its lack of power and reliability. The design later became modified into the highly successful Lancaster four-engine bomber. This perhaps proves how comparatively fine is the dividing line between success and failure in aeroplane design, but it is a sphere where failure can often be fatal.

Flying Officer L. Manser was awarded the V.C. posthumously as captain of a Manchester, flying in the mass raid on Cologne during the night of 30–31 May 1942. It was the first 1,000-bomber raid in history. Despite the enemy defences, he pressed home his attack. But hits hammered regularly on the Manchester. The rear-gunner was wounded; smoke seeped into the front cabin; the port engine over-heated. Then the port engine burst into flames. Although it was extinguished, the engine was out too. The aircraft began to lose height. Manser kept it airborne until each of his crew of six had baled out safely. Then the bomber crashed with Manser still at the controls.

Master (Miles)

Mk II

Engine	One 870 h.p. Bristol Mercury XX radial
Span	39 ft
Length	29 ft 6 ins
Height	9 ft 3 ins
Weight empty	4,293 lb
Weight loaded	5,573 lb
Crew number	Two
Maximum speed	242 m.p.h. at 6,000 ft
Service ceiling	25,100
Normal range	393 miles
Armament	NV

Meteor (Gloster)

Mk III

Engines	Two 2,000 lb s.t. Rolls Royce Derwent turbojets
Span	43 ft
Length	41 ft 4 ins
Height	13 ft
Weight empty	10,519 lb
Weight loaded	13,920 lb
Crew number	One
Maximum speed	415 m.p.h. at 10,000 ft
Service ceiling	40,000 ft
Normal range	NV
Armament	Four 20 mm. Hispano cannon

The Master was a two-seater monoplane advanced trainer and glider-tug. Accommodation was arranged in tandem with dual controls and instructor and trainee pilot. The Master reached the Royal Air Force a few months before war broke out. The Master I had a 715 h.p. Rolls Royce Kestrel XXX engine. The Master II went over to the Bristol Mercury XX engine rated at 870 h.p. This in turn was succeeded by the Master III with an 825 h.p. Pratt and Whitney Wasp Junior engine. The low cantilever monoplane wing of the earlier versions was clipped on the III. Many wartime pilots underwent their advanced training on the Master. Trainers are always destined to be less glamorous, less famous, than their fighter counterparts, but the Master did its job well.

Meteor: Comparison of Marks

		I		III		IV		VIII		XINF	
Span	Ft in.	43	0	43	0	37	2	37	2	43	0
Length	Ft in.	41	3	41	3	41	0	44	7	48	6
Height	Ft in.	13	0	13	0	13	0	13	10	13	10
Weight	Lb	13,795		13,920		14,545		15,700		16,542	
Speed	m.p.h.	415		415		580		598		580	
at	Ft	10,000		10,000		10,000		10,000		10,000	
Ceiling	Ft	40,000		44,000		44,500		43,000		NV	
Range	Miles	NV		NV		NV		NV		NV	

The Meteor was the first Royal Air Force jet fighter and it flew operationally during 1944–45. The original Gloster Whittle jet had first flown as early as May 1941,

39

but more than three years elapsed before the first Meteor actually entered service. This was the Meteor I and its first active operations were to try and combat the V.1 Doodle Bugs. The Meteor was the aircraft concerned in the famous instance of a pilot flying parallel to a V.1 and then destroying it by the unusual means of tipping it off trajectory with a wing of the Meteor. The Meteor I was powered by two 1,700 lb s.t. Rolls Royce W.2B/23 Welland I turbojets. For the Meteor III, two 2,000 lb s.t. Rolls Royce Derwent turbojets were introduced instead. The chief performance characteristic of the Meteor III included a maximum speed of 415 m.p.h. and a high ceiling of 40,000 feet. The range, too, was proportionately further than former fighters, at 1,340 miles. Four 20 mm. cannon provided its fighting power. In 1945 the Meteor was flying over the Continent ready to oppose the enemy's Messerschmitt jet 262. But by then the war in Europe was nearly over. Soon after VJ-Day the Meteor IV established a new air speed record, topping 606 m.p.h. Later Meteors were V, VI and VII, while the VIII flew as a fighter until ten years after the war.

Mitchell (North American)

Mk II (B-25 C/D)

Engines	Two 1,700 h.p. Wright Cyclone R-2600-13
Span	67 ft 7 ins
Length	52 ft 11 ins
Height	15 ft 10 ins
Weight empty	20,300 lb
Weight loaded	34,000 lb
Crew number	Three to six
Maximum speed	284 m.p.h. at 15,000 ft
Service ceiling	21,200 ft
Normal range	1,500 miles
Armament	Six .50 machine guns; up to 5,200 lb of bombs

The Mitchell was a successful twin-engine medium bomber and ground-attack aircraft. It was ordered by the U.S. Army Air Corps and of course made in America. While the Battle of Britain was at its height, the Mitchell B-25 flew for the first time and deliveries to the U.S.A.A.C. started early in 1941. Mass production of the Mitchell proceeded during 1941–42, some 4,000 B-25Cs and B-25Ds being manufactured. About a couple of dozen B-25Bs were delivered to the Royal Air Force

as well, under the British designation of Mitchell I. The purpose of this advance quota was to train crews for the larger-scale deliveries which followed. These were Mitchell IIs, the same aircraft as the quantity-produced American B-25C and B-25D, and Mitchell IIIs, the American B-25J.
Illustration in colour section

Mosquito (de Havilland)

Mk B XVI

Engines	Two 1,680 h.p. Rolls Royce Merlin 72 or 76
Span	54 ft 2 ins
Length	41 ft 6 ins
Height	15 ft 3 ins
Weight empty	14,600
Weight loaded	23,000 lb
Crew number	Two
Maximum speed	415 m.p.h. at 28,000 ft
Service ceiling	40,000 ft
Normal range	1,370 miles
Armament	Up to 4,000 lb of bombs

Mk NF XIX

Engines	Two 1,635 h.p. Rolls Royce Merlin 25 inlines
Span	54 ft 2 ins
Length	40 ft 11 ins
Height	15 ft 3 ins
Weight empty	14,000 lb
Weight loaded	21,750 lb
Crew number	Two
Maximum speed	372 m.p.h. at 13,000 ft
Service ceiling	34,500 ft
Normal range	1,830 miles
Armament	Four 20 mm. Hispano cannon

Mosquito: Comparison of Marks

		NF II	B IV	FB VI	NF XII	NF XIII
Span	Ft in.	54 2	54 2	54 2	54 2	54 2
Length	Ft in.	40 11	40 9	40 6	40 11	40 11
Height	Ft in.	15 3	15 3	15 3	15 3	15 3
Weight	Lb	20,000	20,870	22,300	20,000	20,000
Speed	m.p.h.	370	380	380	370	370
at	Ft	14,000	17,000	13,000	14,000	14,000
Ceiling	Ft	34,500	28,800	36,000	34,500	34,500
Range	Miles	1,860	NV	1,705	1,860	1,860

		B XVI		NF XIX		NF 30		TR 33	
Span	Ft in.	54	2	54	2	54	2	54	2
Length	Ft in.	41	6	41	11	41	9	42	3
Height	Ft in.	15	3	15	3	15	3	13	6
Weight	Lb	23,000		21,750		21,600		22,500	
Speed	m.p.h.		415		372		407		385
at	Ft		28,000		13,000		28,000		13,500
Ceiling	Ft		40,000		34,500		39,000		30,000
Range	Miles		1,370		1,830		1,770		1,260

The Mosquito was conceived as far back as 1938, to be constructed entirely of wood. This was one of its unique qualities. Another was the sheer versatility of this exciting aircraft. Although planned originally as a bomber dependent on speed instead of any defensive weaponry, the Mosquito later became a bomber from both high and low altitudes; a fighter equally valuable by day or night; and almost everything in-between: fighter-bomber, Pathfinder, mine-layer, ground attack, shipping strike, photo reconnaissance, trainer and transport, as Kenneth Munson rightly observes in his *Aircraft of World War II*. The unarmed bomber made its first flight in November 1940, hurried through trials in three months, and joined the R.A.F. in July 1941. A fighter version was developed, too, as well as the PR Mosquito. The Mosquito I was powered by two Rolls Royce Merlin XXI engines. Only ten of these were built. The F II fighter had XXI, XXII or XXIII engines, four 20 mm. cannons and four .303 Browning guns. This home defence version operated from April 1942. The III was a two-seat trainer. The B IV was the unarmed bomber fitted to carry four 500 lb bombs. Cologne was raided by Mosquitoes on 31 May 1942 and Berlin by daylight on 30 January 1943. Some other IVs had conversions to carry a 4,000 lb bomb. The Pathfinder Mosquito was a IV with special radar, and it went into service in 1942. There was also a PR IV with cameras instead of bombs. The V had wings which could take extra fuel tanks or bomb load. The VI was the fighter-bomber with a maximum load of 2,000 lb which saw action by 1943 in areas as far apart as Europe and Burma. This mark, with rocket projectiles under the wings, flew for Coastal Command against enemy shipping with success. The VIII became the first high-altitude version, but only five were constructed. It had Merlin 61 engines. The B IX was the first actual high-level unarmed bomber powered by Merlin 72 engines. This could carry a 4,000 lb bomb. Mosquito IXs made their first daylight raid on Germany with these bombs when they attacked Duisberg on 29 November 1944. Pathfinder IX version had special radar fitted. The maximum speed of this mark topped 400 m.p.h. and it had a still-air range of 1,500 miles with

a ceiling of 36,000 feet – a formidable combination. The PR IX could fly for 2,000 miles. The NF XII was a night-fighter with four cannon and AI radar, later replaced by the XIII. The NF XV was a high-level fighter, adapted at top urgency in exactly one week! Mosquitoes were also made in Canada. The aircraft continued to be developed for years after the war, to mark T.43. Total wartime production was 6,710.

Group Captain Leonard Cheshire received the V.C. after completing one hundred bombing missions, many in Lancasters. The raid for which he was actually awarded the V.C. took place on 24 April 1944 against Munich, though on this occasion he was leading four Mosquitoes to mark the target with flares. Cheshire flew over Munich at 1,000 feet in the earlier stages of the attack and as the bombs were falling. His aircraft was hit and damaged by shell fragments, but he continued to direct operations. Only when he could do no more did he set course for base. As a leader of Pathfinder forces, his aircraft was always very vulnerable to enemy attack.

Illustration in colour section

Mustang (North American)

Mustang IV

Engine	One 1,490 h.p. Rolls-Royce Packard Merlin V-1,650-7 inline
Span	37 ft 0¼ ins
Length	32 ft 3 ins
Height	13 ft 8 ins
Weight empty	7,125 lb
Weight loaded	11,600 lb (maximum)
Crew number	One
Maximum speed	437 m.p.h. at 25,000 ft
Service ceiling	41,900 ft
Maximum range	2,300 miles
Armament	Six .50 machine guns; or four .50 machine guns and up to 2,000 lb of bombs or ten 5 in. rockets

The Mustang was a long-range escort or pursuit aeroplane and has been called the most effective American fighter of the Second World War, or more alliteratively, the perfect pursuit plane. This low-wing monoplane had strange Anglo-American parentage. In April 1940, Britain asked the makers to produce a fighter

Below right: The Oxford was used as an advanced trainer and flying ambulance

Right: Seafire Mk IB about to land on HMS *Formidable*.
Below right: Seafire Mk III overrunning arrester wires and crashing into barrier

in quantity for the R.A.F. and the first flight of the prototype was in September 1940. Delivery of over 600 models of this Mustang I started in October 1941. Its visual features included the low, square-cut wing configuration, two .50 machine guns in the nose and two more, together with four .30 machine guns, in the wings. By 1942 Britain and the U.S. had agreed to a suggestion of cross-breeding the high-altitude Mustang fighter with the Rolls Royce Merlin engine. Two variants went into bulk production and some 900 Mustang IIIs (American P-51 Bs and Cs) were made for the R.A.F. These were followed by the P-51D production of 7,956 – including 875 Mustang IVs for the R.A.F.

The original Mustangs first went into action with the R.A.F. from July 1942, and flew in the North African campaign during the winter of 1942–43. Later they were used for artillery spotting high over the Salerno beaches of Italy in September 1943. The P-51D or Mustang IV arrived in Britain by 1944, featuring a plastic bubble or blister canopy for wider-angle vision by the pilot. The Mustang IV equipped sixteen R.A.F. squadrons. Although the Americans took practically all the production of this P-51D, the fighter carried out good work with the R.A.F. over Europe, where its 437 m.p.h. top speed, 2,300 miles maximum range and eight hours' endurance were all valuable.

Oxford (Airspeed)

Mk I

Engines	Two 375 h.p. Armstrong-Siddeley Cheetah X radials
Span	53 ft 4 ins
Length	34 ft 6 ins
Height	11 ft 1 in.
Weight empty	5,380 lb
Weight loaded	7,600 lb
Crew number	Three
Maximum speed	182 m.p.h. at 8,300 ft
Service ceiling	19,500 ft
Normal range	925 miles

The Oxford was one of the more valuable, yet lesser known aircraft in operation throughout the war; doubling as an advanced trainer and a flying ambulance. By 1939, the Oxford had already become established as the R.A.F.'s very first training monoplane with two engines. This Oxford I was powered by two 375 h.p. Armstrong-Siddeley Cheetah X radials, and it acted in a training capacity for both gunnery and bombing crews. Unlike the I, the II had no gun turret, being equipped for the role of pilot and radio and navigation trainer. The III switched to two 425 h.p. Cheetah XV engines and had a role similar to the II. Only one Oxford IV

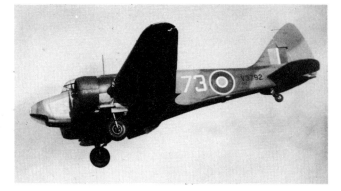

was ever produced, used as a flying test-bed for new engines. The last Oxford, V, had two 450 h.p. Pratt and Whitney Wasp Junior nine-cylinder radial air-cooled engines and was used mainly overseas for navigation and radio training. As well as its training and ambulance duties, the Oxford also flew on anti-aircraft co-operation sorties. Known in the R.A.F., but unsung by the world at large.

Seafire (Supermarine)

Mk III F

Engine	One 1,470 h.p. Rolls Royce Merlin 55 inline
Span	36 ft 8 ins
Length	30 ft
Height	11 ft 2 ins
Weight empty	5,400 lb
Weight loaded	7,100 lb
Crew number	One
Maximum speed	352 m.p.h. at 12,250 ft
Service ceiling	33,800 ft
Normal range	725 miles
Armament	Two 20 mm. cannon and four .303 machine guns; one 500 lb or two 250 lb bombs.

Seafire: Comparison of Marks

		I B		LII C		F III		FR III		XV	
Span	Ft in.	36	8	36	8	36	8	36	8	36	10
Length	Ft in.	30	0	30	0	30	0	30	0	32	3
Height	Ft in.	11	2	11	2	11	2	11	2	10	8
Weight	Lb	6,700		7,000		7,100		7,200		8,000	
Speed	m.p.h.	365		333		352		341		383	
at	Ft	16,000		5,000		12,250		6,000		13,500	
Ceiling	Ft	36,400		32,000		33,800		31,500		35,500	
Range	Miles	770		755		725		771		640	

		XV II		45		46		47	
Span	Ft in.	36	10	36	11	36	11	36	11
Length	Ft in.	32	3	33	7	33	7	34	4
Height	Ft in.	10	8	12	9	12	9	12	9
Weight	Lb	8,000		9,400		9,730		11,615	
Speed	m.p.h.	387		438		NV		452	
at	Ft	13,500		25,000		NV		20,500	
Ceiling	Ft	35,200		41,000		NV		43,100	
Range	Miles	860		740		NV		940	

The Seafire was the Royal Navy's version of the R.A.F.'s Spitfire, suitably converted for use from aircraft-carriers. The original trials to test out the validity of the idea were successfully carried out in 1941, using an adapted Spitfire V B. The basic distinction between the Spitfire and Seafire I B, as it became, was the deck-arrester hook. The Seafire was powered by a Rolls Royce Merlin engine of various marks. The next development was the II C, adapted from the Spitfire V C. The Seafire III proved to be of prominent importance and over a thousand were manufactured. Not only did it fly as a naval fighter at 352 m.p.h., but it also assumed a photographic-reconnaissance role as well. This version introduced the

folding wing capacity, taking the fold beyond the vertical and hinging the tips outwards so that they were horizontal. It was also made with clipped wings, as opposed to the normal span, and could carry up to 500 lb of bombs. Next, there was a jump in nomenclature to the Seafire XV, the first to be powered by a Griffon engine. This was the 1,850 h.p. Griffon VI. By the time the aeroplane had entered service, VE-Day had come and gone, but the Seafire XV served with U.K.-based squadrons before VJ day. Like the Spitfire, the Seafire continued post-war development and production, from the XVII in September 1945 to the 47 version which actually served with success in Korea. The date of the Seafire's final retirement was late-1954.

Sea Hurricane (Hawker)

Mk I A

Engine	One Rolls Royce Merlin II or III 1,030 h.p. engine
Span	40 ft
Length	32 ft
Height	13 ft 1 in.
Weight empty	6,600 lb
Crew number	One
Maximum speed	318 m.p.h.
Service ceiling	32,000 ft
Maximum range	490 miles
Armament	Light .303 Browning machine guns in wings

The Sea Hurricane had the distinction of being the first single-seat monoplane fighter to fly to and from Royal Navy aircraft-carriers. The aeroplane was essentially the Hurricane fitted with catapult spools and deck-arrester gear in the form of a hook. They were known as

Right: Sea Hurricane Mk IB was the first single-seat aeroplane to use a Royal Navy aircraft carrier. **Below right**: Sea Hurricane Mk IA being catapulted off a merchant ship

Hurricats. The original fifty Sea Hurricanes were not in fact fitted with the deck-arrester gear. They were manufactured at short notice to be flown from catapult-equipped merchantmen – CAM ships. This idea went into operation in spring 1941 to defend convoys against long-range enemy air attack. Frequently, however, after attacking the enemy the Hurricat pilot had no alternative but to ditch the aeroplane and hope to be rescued by the convoy. This Sea Hurricane I A had its first success against the enemy aircraft on 3 August 1941. The I B was the first fitted with both catapult spools and deck-arrester gear for operation on an aircraft-carrier. The I C was similar but with Hurricane II C four-cannon wings. The I B went into operation in the Mediterranean in the summer of 1942, and its most memorable action dated from August 1942, when seventy aircraft including Fulmars, Martlets and Sea Hurricanes defended one of the famous Malta convoys for some seventy-two hours against hundreds of enemy aircraft. The original Sea Hurricane had a Rolls Royce Merlin II or III engine of 1,030 h.p. The Sea Hurricane II B and II C introduced the Merlin XX 1,280 h.p. engine, while the Sea Hurricane XII had a Packard Merlin 29 engine.

Skua (Blackburn)

Mk II

Engine	One 890 h.p. Bristol Perseus XII
Span	46 ft 2 ins
Length	35 ft 7 ins
Height	12 ft 6 ins
Weight loaded	8,228 lbs (dive bomber) 8,124 lbs (fighter)
Crew number	Two
Maximum speed	225 m.p.h. at 6,500 ft
Service ceiling	19,100 ft (dive bomber) 20,200 ft (fighter)
Normal range	760 miles
Armament	Five machine guns one 500 lb bomb

The Skua was one of those aircraft little-remembered among the more illustrious names in both land and sea spheres. It was actually quite famous in its day as being the first aeroplane of the Fleet Air Arm to shoot down an enemy during the war. The Skua was a fighter dive-bomber, in service when war broke out. The first monoplane ever to become operational with the Fleet Air Arm, the Skua had its moment of glory and then gradually faded. When the war was two years old, it began to be withdrawn from the combat role, yet flew in the capacity of training and target-towing for the rest

Below: The Skua. It was the first Fleet Air Arm aeroplane to shoot down an enemy

of the war. The Mk II was powered by a single 890 h.p. Bristol Perseus XII radial engine, which gave it a top speed of 225 m.p.h. Visually, its distinctive feature was the low-slung wing and large cockpit.

Spitfire (Supermarine)

Mk V B

Engine	One 1,440 h.p. Rolls Royce Merlin 45 inline
Span	36 ft 10 ins
Length	29 ft 11 ins
Height	11 ft 5 ins
Weight empty	5,065 lb
Weight loaded	6,650 lb
Crew number	One
Maximum speed	374 m.p.h. at 13,000 ft
Service ceiling	37,000 ft
Normal range	1,135 miles
Armament	Two 20 mm. cannon and four .303 machine guns, one 500 lb or two 250 lb bombs

Mk XIV

Engine	One 2,050 h.p. Rolls Royce Griffon 65 inline
Span	36 ft 10 ins
Length	32 ft 8 ins
Height	12 ft 8 ins
Weight empty	6,600 lb
Weight loaded	8,500 lb
Crew number	One
Maximum speed	448 m.p.h. at 26,000 ft
Service ceiling	44,500 ft
Normal range	850 miles
Armament	Two 20 mm. cannon and four .303 machine guns; up to 1,000 lb of bombs

Spitfire: Comparison of Marks

		I	II	III	IV	V A
Span	Ft in.	36 10	36 10	36 10	36 10	36 10
	Ft in.					32 2
Length	Ft in.	29 11	29 11	29 11	29 11	29 11
Height	Ft in.	11 5	11 5	11 5	11 5	11 5
Weight	Lb	5,784	6,527	NV	7,178	6,417
Speed	m.p.h.	355	357	NV	372	374
	m.p.h.					357
at	Ft	19,000	17,000	NV	NV	13,000
	Ft					6,000
Ceiling	Ft	34,000	37,200	NV	39,600	37,000
	Ft					36,500
Range	Miles	NV	500	NV	NV	1,135

		V B	V C	VI	VII	F VIII
Span	Ft in.	36 10	36 10	40 2	40 2	32 2
	Ft in.	32 2	32 2			
Length	Ft in.	29 11	29 11	29 11	31 0	30 4
Height	Ft in.	11 5	11 5	NV	NV	NV
Weight	Lb	6,650	6,785	6,797	7,875	7,767
Speed	m.p.h.	374	374	364	408	408
	m.p.h.	357	357			
at	Ft	13,000	13,000	NV	25,000	25,000
	Ft	6,000	6,000			
Ceiling	Ft	37,000	37,000	NV	43,000	43,000
	Ft	36,500	36,500			
Range	Miles	1,135	1,135	NV	1,180	NV

		LF VIII	HF VIII	HF IX	LF IX	X
Span	Ft in.	36 10	40 2	36 10	32 2	NV
Length	Ft in.	30 4	30 4	31 4	30 6	NV
Height	Ft in.	NV	NV	11 5	11 5	NV
Weight	Lb	7,767	7,767	7,500	7,500	8,159
Speed	m.p.h.	404	416	416	404	416
at	Ft	21,000	27,500	27,500	21,000	NV
Ceiling	Ft	41,500	44,000	45,000	42,500	NV
Range	Miles	NV	1,180	980	980	900

		XI	XII	XIII	XIV	XVI
Span	Ft in.	36 10	32 7	NV	36 10	32 8
Length	Ft in.	31 4	31 10	NV	32 8	31 4
Height	Ft in.	NV	NV	NV	12 8	12 7⅜
Weight	Lb	7,900	7,400	NV	8,500	7,500
Speed	m.p.h.	422	393	400	448	405
at	Ft	NV	18,000	NV	26,000	22,000
Ceiling	Ft	NV	40,000	NV	44,500	40,500
Range	Miles	2,000	493	700	850	980

		XVIII	XIX	XX
Span	Ft in.	36 10	36 10	36 10
Length	Ft in.	33 3¼	32 8	30 6
Height	Ft in.	NV	12 8	NV
Weight	Lb	9,320	9,000	NV
Speed	m.p.h.	442	460	NV
at	Ft	NV	NV	NV
Ceiling	Ft	41,000	43,000	NV
Range	Miles	NV	1,550	NV

		XXI	XXII	XXIV
Span	Ft in.	36 11	36 11	36 11
Length	Ft ins	32 8	32 11	32 11
Height	Ft in.	NV	NV	NV

Weight	Lb	9,200	9,900	9,900
Speed	m.p.h.	454	454	454
at	Ft	26,000	26,000	26,000
Ceiling	Ft	43,500	43,500	NV
Range	Miles	880	880	NV

The Spitfire has become synonymous with the Battle of Britain. The perfect complement to the Hurricane, the Spitfire defeated the enemy in this most decisive air conflict of history, and one of the most momentous battles of all time. Designed by R. J. Mitchell, the Spitfire was the sole Allied fighter to be in production throughout the war. The prototype flew first on 5 March 1936, and its top speed of 349 m.p.h. placed it at once as the fastest fighter in the world. The Spitfire was an all-metal, low-wing cantilever monoplane with retractable landing gear, and the prototype was powered by one of the first Rolls Royce Merlin engines. The Spitfire I had a Merlin II or III engine and its two-blade wood fixed-pitch airscrew was later superseded by a three-blade variable pitch, duralumin airscrew. The fighter was armed with eight .303 machine guns, and subsequently with two 20 mm. cannon and four .303 machine guns.

The Spitfire joined the R.A.F. in 1938 and was in service with nine squadrons by September 1939. Spitfires shot down the first enemy aircraft over Britain since the First World War. The Spitfire II went into production powered by the Merlin XII engine of 1,175 h.p. Over 3,000 of the Spitfire I and II were made altogether. After the Battle of Britain, it was the Spitfire II that launched the 'Rhubarb' sweeps over Europe. The Spitfire IV met the requirement for a reconnaissance aeroplane of formidable speed. This was powered by the Merlin 45. It carried cameras and extra oxygen but no armament. The Spitfire V was one of the best-known marks, also powered by the 1,440 h.p. Merlin 46. Its extra assets included a clearer windscreen and special tropical equipment, as well as drop tanks. It operated from summer 1941 and was the first Spitfire to serve beyond Britain. But the main claim of the V was as the first-line machine of Fighter Command through 1941 and 1942. Much later, in 1943, the Spitfire V had its wings clipped, literally, as a low-level fighter, and provision was made for it to carry two 250 or one 500 lb bomb. The Spitfire VI with Merlin 47 featured a pressure cabin for high-level flying. The Spitfire VII had the Merlin 61 engine and, like the VI, had extended wingtips yielding a span of 40 ft 2 ins. It was another high-level design and the more powerful engine enabled it to exceed 400 m.p.h. for the first time. The Spitfire VIII was designed to take the Merlin 61 engine and its aim was to counter the formidable Focke Wulf FW 190 fighter, whose speed was greater than earlier Spitfires. The IX was an adaptation of the VC using the same engine, and production of the Spitfire IX exceeded 5,000 aircraft.

The Spitfire X and XI were both long-range photo reconnaissance versions, the latter capable of up to 2,000 miles. The XI was, in fact, the principal aircraft of Coastal Command's photo-reconnaissance unit from then on. The first version with the Rolls Royce Griffon III or IV engine was the Spitfire XII, used to counter the Focke Wulf's switch to the low-level offensive role. The major Griffon variant was the Spitfire XIV with its 2,050 h.p. Griffon 65 engine. This went into service in 1944 and was responsible for the destruction of more than 300 V.I. flying bombs – as well as being the first R.A.F. aircraft to shoot down a German jet Me 262. Its maximum performance was at high level. Other refinements included a propeller of five blades and sliding 'bubble hoods' with improved rear vision for the pilot. The Spitfire XVI was powered by the Packard-built Merlin 266 engine. This was flown with normal 36 ft 10 in wings and clipped wings and like many of the later marks, it could carry bombs. This was the last version to be made in a quantity exceeding 1,000. The final distinguished wartime Spitfire was the XIX photo-reconnaissance edition of the XIV. It had a ceiling altitude of 43,000 feet and a top speed of 460 m.p.h. – at least 100 m.p.h. faster than the original Spitfires. The Spitfire went up to Mk XXIV after the war, the very last one emerging in 1947. Total production over the decade of its manufacture topped 20,000. The Spitfire was probably the most famous fighter aircraft ever made.

Illustration in colour section

Stirling (Short)

Mk I

Engines	Four 1,590 h.p. Bristol Hercules XI radials
Span	99 ft 1 in.
Length	87 ft 3 ins
Height	22 ft 9 ins
Weight empty	44,000 lb
Weight loaded	59,400 lb
Crew number	Seven or eight
Maximum speed	260 m.p.h. at 10,500 ft
Service ceiling	20,500 ft
Maximum range	2,330 miles
Armament	Eight .303 Browning machine guns; up to 14,000 lb of bombs

Stirling: Comparison of Marks

		I		II		III	
Span	Ft in.	99	1	99	1	99	1
Length	Ft in.	87	3	87	3	87	3
Height	Ft in.	22	9	22	9	22	9
Weight	Lb	59,400		59,400		70,000	
Speed	m.p.h.	260		NV		270	
at	Ft	10,500		NV		14,500	
Ceiling	Ft	NV		NV		17,000	
Range	Miles	2,330		NV		2,010	

The Stirling was a heavy bomber – in fact the first four-engine bomber to join the Royal Air Force. Its prototype flew first in May 1939, but it had the misfortune to crash when landing from this maiden flight. Despite the setback, another prototype was in the air soon after war broke out. The first production Stirling I joined the R.A.F. at the time of the Battle of Britain in August 1940. It was powered by four 1,590 h.p. Bristol Hercules XI radial engines and had no dorsal turret. It could carry a considerable bomb load of 14,000 lb and needed a crew of seven or eight. The Stirling I went into the bombing attack first on the night of 10–11 February 1941. It was also used for daylight raids, but within a year it had been allocated predominantly for night-bombing. After a few Stirling IIs were built with four Wright Cyclone engines from the United States, the Stirling III went into production with four 1,650 h.p. Bristol Hercules VI or XVI engines. This version also added a mid-upper turret and it was subsequently equipped for towing gliders. Its days as a bomber were numbered, however, with the Lancaster and Halifax achieving more prominence and success. The Stirling IV was, in fact, a long-range troop transport, as well as a tug to tow the Horsa glider. Provision was made to drop paratroops from this edition. The last Stirling, the V, was an unarmed military transport and freighter version of the Stirling III, with a stretched nose. Its range of just on 3,000 miles was one of the longest of any R.A.F. aeroplanes then in service.

Illustration in colour section

Flight Sergeant R. Middleton was awarded the V.C. posthumously for his part in a raid against the Fiat Works at Turin on 28 November 1942. Seven Stirlings formed the force. Over the target, a shell struck the cockpit, shattered the windscreen and wounded both pilots. Middleton's right eye was destroyed and he was also wounded in the body and legs. The Stirling started to go down, but they managed to drop their bombs. Then they set course for England, facing an Alpine crossing with most of the crew wounded, in a badly damaged aircraft – and without enough fuel. Middleton's wounds worsened, but his aim was to try and reach the English coast. For eight hours he had kept up the Stirling and himself. Nearing the Kent coast, the fuel was virtually gone. He told the crew to bale out. Five survived, two perished. Middleton and the Stirling crashed into the sea off Dymchurch.

Flight Sergeant A. Aaron was also awarded the V.C. posthumously for his action in a Stirling, on 12 August 1943. Near the target of Turin, three engines were hit; the windscreen was shattered; turrets were put out of action, and other damage sustained. The navigator was killed and others wounded. Aaron's jaw was broken, he was wounded in the lung, and his right arm was rendered useless. He urged the bomb-aimer to take over the controls after the Stirling had dived several thousand feet. Five hours from Turin, they sighted the flare path of Bone, North Africa. With Aaron's help, the bomb-aimer brought the bomber in for a landing at the fifth attempt. Nine hours later, Aaron died from exhaustion.

Sunderland (Short)

Mk V

Engines	Four 1,200 h.p. Pratt and Whitney Twin Wasp R-1830 radials
Span	112 ft 10 ins
Length	85 ft 4 ins
Height	32 ft 10 ins
Weight empty	37,000 lb
Weight loaded	60,000 lb
Crew number	Thirteen
Maximum speed	213 m.p.h. at 5,000 ft
Service ceiling	17,900 ft
Normal range	2,980 miles
Armament	Two .50 and eight or twelve .303 machine guns; up to 2,000 lb of bombs.

Sunderland: Comparison of Marks

		I	II	III	V
Span	Ft in.	112 10	112 10	112 10	112 10
Length	Ft in.	85 4	85 4	85 4	85 4
Height	Ft in.	NV	NV	NV	32 10
Weight	Lb	50,100	58,000	58,000	60,000
Speed	m.p.h.	210	205	205	213
at	Ft	NV	NV	NV	5,000
Ceiling	Ft	NV	NV	NV	17,900
Range	Miles	NV	NV	NV	2,980

continued on page 97

COLOUR
SECTION

Seafire fighters

The Albacore torpedo bomber
Left : Loading torpedo
Below : Bombing up

Oxford (left) and Fairey Battle (right)
The Oxford's upper fuselage gunner is practising
on a target towed by the Battle

Beaufighters in the desert (right) and flying over Malta (below). Beaufighters were used primarily as night fighters

Beauforts in flight and in Malta (left). The Beaufort was a torpedo and reconnaissance bomber

Bostons were used as trainers, night fighters and
day bombers

Left: Boston with nose machine gunner, showing
open bomb bay
Below: Harvard trainers in formation
Overleaf: Halifax heavy bomber

Hudson maritime reconnaissance bomber in the Far East

Hurricane Mark IIs in desert

Top: Hurricane Mk IID attacking tank in Tunisia
Bottom: Mk I Hurricane being serviced
Overleaf: Lancasters in factory

The Lancaster was Britain's most illustrious heavy bomber
Left: Maintenance
Right: King George VI inspecting ground crew
Overleaf: In flight

The Mosquito (right) filled a variety of roles
including light bomber, fighter, mine-layer and
photo-reconnaissance aircraft
Below left: Mosquitoes of No 139 Squadron
Below right: Bombing up a Mosquito BIV with
500 lb bombs

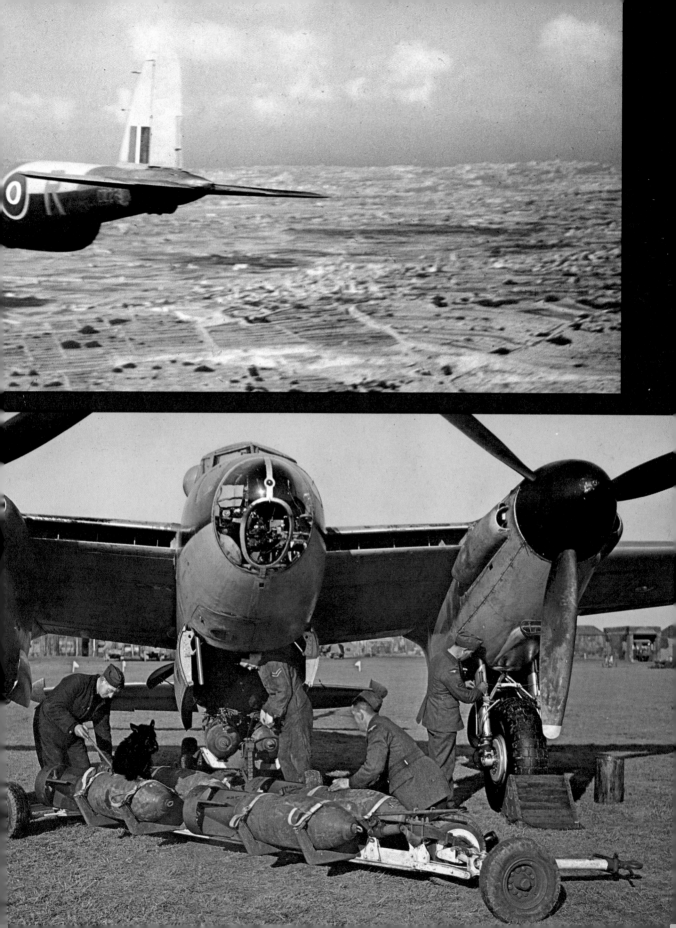

Mosquito BIV aircraft in formation
Previous pages: Mosquitoes of R.A.F. Coastal
Command take off on dawn raid

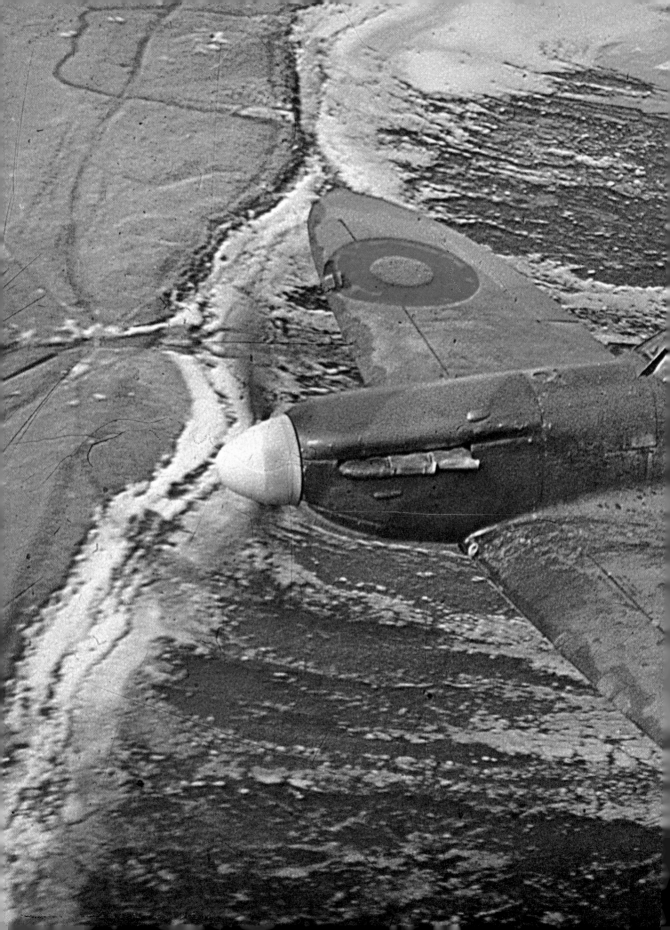

Previous pages: Spitfire Mk II
Above: Spitfire Mk Vb in desert

Spitfires Mk Vc

Spitfires Mk IXc over Italy

The Stirling was the R.A.F.'s first heavy bomber
Left: Bombing up

The Sunderland was used for maritime patrol and
anti-submarine duties

The Typhoon was a ground attack rocket-firing aircraft which could also carry bombs

Below: Bomb load for the Wellington, Britain's leading twin-engined medium bomber
Left: The Whitley was the first of the twin-engined bombers

Wildcats—carrier-borne fighters on H.M.S. Formidable

Reference Section: *continued from page 48*

The Sunderland was to all intents and purposes a military version of the then famous Empire flying-boats in use during the later 1930s. The Sunderland ran a year or so behind the Empire boat and by 1939 there were three squadrons equipped with them. Carrying a crew of thirteen, the Sunderland kept the double-decker Empire design to house this considerable number of crew. The Sunderland I had four Bristol Pegasus 22 engines and, although conceived for maritime patrol and reconnaissance, it found itself used as a troop transport in various Allied evacuations familiar to the first year or two of the war. The Sunderland II utilised four Pegasus XVIII engines and was flying late in 1941. It also had a two-gun dorsal turret instead of manually-operated guns. The III sported a streamlined hull and proved to be the principal production edition. The Sunderland V had four 1,200 h.p. Pratt and Whitney Twin Wasp radial engines. This flying boat had the huge span of 112 feet and a range of 2,980 miles, making it one of the longest-range craft of its era. Among its most vital successes were the sinking of many enemy U-boats, and six years' versatile service gave it a claim to unique aviation fame. Visually, this flying hotel had high-set wings which emphasised its overall height of nearly 33 feet.

Illustration in colour section

Swordfish (Fairey)

Mk I

Engine	One 690 h.p. Bristol Pegasus III M.3 radial
Span	45 ft 6 ins
Length	36 ft 4 ins
Height	12 ft 10 ins
Weight empty	5,200 lb
Weight loaded	9,250 lb
Crew number	Two or three
Maximum speed	139 m.p.h. at 4,750 ft
Service ceiling	10,700 ft
Normal range	546 miles
Armament	Two .303 machine guns; one 1,610 lb torpedo, one 1,500 lb mine or equivalent load of bombs

The Swordfish was designed originally as a torpedo-spotter reconnaissance aeroplane for operation from aircraft carriers of the Fleet Air Arm. It was a famous biplane and went into naval service in 1936. In normal times it would have been nearing its natural age of obsolescence by 1939. But with the war, the Swordfish squadrons assumed vital importance and began to serve in a progressive number of roles – as torpedo-bombers, anti-U-boat aircraft, shore-based mine-layers, rocket-projectile-carriers, flare-droppers, and trainers. The Swordfish I had a single reliable 690 h.p. Bristol Pegasus III M.3 radial engine and carried a crew of two or three. The II was powered by the same engine, or a slightly stronger 750 h.p. Bristol Pegasus XXX. It was the Swordfish II which was equipped to carry rocket projectiles. The III had radar added. Wherever sea battles were fought, Swordfish seemed to be there. They helped to mutilate the Italians in the Battle of Taranto; they flew with gallantry in half a dozen other Mediterranean areas; they figured largely in the Battle of Matapan off the Greek coast, and did not let their slow speed of 139 m.p.h. interfere with their destined role in the destruction of the *Bismarck*. Swordfish operating from Malta sank some 50,000 tons of Axis vessels monthly. Blackburn and Fairey both produced quantities of Swordfish, and this last example of the operational biplane continued being manufactured until after D-Day. The Swordfish served from the Atlantic to Greece, from 1939–45.

Illustration in colour section

Lieutenant Commander E. Esmonde led the six Swordfish on 12 February 1942 which attacked the *Scharnhorst*, *Gneisenau* and *Prinz Eugen* escaping from Brest via the English Channel to a safer port. The pilots were told: 'Fly at 50 feet; close line astern. Individual attacks. Find your own way home.' None of the Swordfish survived the onslaught from the three battleships, escorting screen of ships, or accompanying Me 109s and Focke Wulf 190s. Flying in at zero feet, Esmonde was attacked by a Focke Wulf, which loosed a stream of fire from its guns and completely destroyed the upper mainplane of the Swordfish. Esmonde and his crew spun into the sea, never to be seen again. He was awarded the V.C. posthumously. Thirteen men perished and five survived.

Tempest (Hawker)

Mk V

Engine	One 2,180 h.p. Napier Sabre IIA, B or C
Span	41 ft
Length	33 ft 8 ins
Height	16 ft 1 in.
Weight empty	9,000 lb
Weight loaded	11,500 lb

		Crew number	One
		Maximum speed	436 m.p.h. at 18,500 ft
		Service ceiling	36,500 ft
		Maximum range	1,530 miles
		Armament	Four 20 mm. Hispano cannon; two 1,000 lb bombs or eight rockets.

Tempest: Comparison of Marks

		II		V		VI	
Span	Ft in.	41	0	41	0	41	0
Length	Ft in.	34	5	33	8	33	10
Height	Ft in.	15	10	16	1	16	1
Weight	Lb	11,500		11,540		11,700	
Speed	m.p.h.		442		436		438
at	Ft		15,200		18,500		17,800
Ceiling	Ft		37,500		36,000		38,000
Range	Miles		1,640		1,530		1,560

The Tempest was a fighter and fighter-bomber described as a progressive development of the Typhoon, although more accurately arising out of two projects – the Typhoon and the Tornado. The latter had ceased manufacture before reaching real service stage. The Tempest V flew in September 1942. The Tempest I and II in February and June 1943 respectively. The Tempest I had a Sabre IV engine and production was not pursued beyond prototype stage. In the event, the Tempest V turned out to be the first model to go into production, having flown that much earlier than the I and II. The V incorporated the already proved Sabre II engine and flew into service some ten months after its first appearance off the production line. So in April 1944 it was reported in actual action against the enemy. It achieved its most spectacular successes, not against manned adversaries, but as a means of helping to wipe out whole hosts of the hated Doodle Bugs in the summer of 1944. The figure quoted was 638 V.Is destroyed by Tempests. The fighter also met and shot down a score or so of the new Messerschmitt jet fighter, the 262. The Tempest II was built during the war but did not see war service. The Tempest was one of the fastest aircraft in the Second World War, with a top speed of 436 m.p.h.

Typhoon (Hawker)

Mk IB

Engine	One 2,180 h.p. Napier Sabre IIA inline
Span	41 ft 7 ins
Length	31 ft 10 ins
Height	14 ft 10 ins
Weight empty	8,840 lb
Weight loaded	11,700 lb
Crew number	One
Maximum speed	404 m.p.h. at 10,000 ft
Service ceiling	35,200 ft
Maximum range	980 miles
Armament	Four 20 mm. Hispano cannon; two 500 lb or 1,000 lb bombs, or eight rocket projectiles

The Typhoon was a fighter and ground-attack aeroplane with the distinction of being the first to fly operationally, powered by the 2,180 h.p. Napier Sabre IIA engine. The first production model flew in May 1941 and began to be accelerated to try and counter the speed of the Focke Wulf 190. The Typhoon had a top speed of 404 m.p.h., as opposed to the FW 190's 408 m.p.h. Armed with four 20 mm. cannon, the Typhoon IB successfully fought the FW 190 and other enemy aircraft. The fighter could be fitted with racks for a pair of 500 lb or even 1,000 lb bombs – one attached to each wing. Drop tanks could also be fitted to give it additional range. In the long run, however, it was as a rocket-projectile-firing, ground-attack fighter that the Typhoon really scored. This purpose proved ideal for its flying qualities. Each of its eight rockets carried 60 lb of high explosive or else a 25 lb armour-piercing nose. This sort of armament made it lethal against enemy tanks or in train-busting, and the Typhoon gave great support to the Allied armies by knocking out hundreds of tanks after D-Day until the crossing of the Rhine.

Illustration in colour section

Ventura (Lockheed)

Mk II

Engines	Two 2,000 h.p. Pratt and Whitney Double Wasp radials
Span	65 ft 6 ins
Length	51 ft 5 ins
Height	11 ft 11 ins
Weight empty	17,275 lb
Weight loaded	27,250 lb
Crew number	Four
Maximum speed	315 m.p.h. at 15,200 ft
Service ceiling	24,000 ft
Normal range	950 miles
Armament	Eight .50 machine guns; up to 2,500 lb of bombs, or depth charges

The Ventura was a twin-engine patrol-bomber. It looked rather like the Hudson, and in fact followed on from that design. Both were, of course, American. The Ventura I joined the Royal Air Force in 1942, powered by two 2,000 h.p. Pratt and Whitney Double Wasp radial engines. November 1942 marked the start of its operational career with Bomber Command. The following year the Ventura was withdrawn from Bomber Command and entered service with Coastal Command. The Ventura could carry up to 2,500 lb of bombs, or was equipped to drop a torpedo or depth charges in the naval role. There was a certain amount of switching around of Venturas between Britain and the U.S. forces. The U.S. Navy version of the Ventura was designated PV-1, and some of this same type later flew with the Royal Air Force, bearing the nomenclature Ventura IV or V. The aeroplane carried a four-man crew and boasted the respectable top speed of 315 m.p.h.

Squadron Leader L. Trent won the V.C. on 3 May 1943 for leading his Ventura squadron in a daylight raid aimed at the Amsterdam power station. The dozen Venturas were escorted by fighters. Unfortunately, the fighters reached the target too early and had to be recalled to base. This left the Venturas at the mercy of 15–20 Messerschmitts throughout their approach to the target. Six Venturas were destroyed in four minutes. One had already been forced to return to base. Soon only four were still airborne, but then two more went down on the outskirts of the city. A Messerschmitt sent another one spiralling down, so that only Trent's Ventura remained. The Ventura was hit and broke up. Two of the crew died, but Trent and his navigator were hurled clear of the crash and taken prisoner.

Walrus (Supermarine)

Mk II

Engine	One 775 h.p. Bristol Pegasus VI radial
Span	45 ft 10 ins
Length	37 ft 3 ins
Height	15 ft 3 ins
Weight empty	4,900 lb
Weight loaded	7,200 lb
Crew number	Three
Maximum speed	135 m.p.h. at 4,750 ft
Service ceiling	18,500 ft
Normal range	600 miles
Armament	Two or three Vickers K machine guns, with provision for light bombs under wings

The Walrus was an amphibious biplane flying boat of almost archaic lines, which somehow served throughout the Second World War! It joined the Fleet Air Arm in 1936 as an A.B.R. (amphibian-boat-reconnaissance) to be catapulted from all Royal Navy vessels fitted for the purpose. Its role soon developed to spotter, reconnaissance patrol, air/sea rescue, communications

and training. The main difference between the Walrus I and II was that the I had a metal hull, whereas the II was wooden and built by Saunders Roe. Its distinguishing feature was the unique location of the Bristol Pegasus engine above and behind the crew quarters. The Walrus flew in literally all spheres – from the Greenland area to Hong Kong – and despite its limited specifications, managed to perform almost limitless tasks.

Wellington (Vickers)

Mk X

Engines	Two 1,675 h.p. Bristol Hercules VI radials
Span	86 ft 2 ins
Length	64 ft 7 ins
Height	17 ft 6 ins
Weight empty	22,474 lb
Weight loaded	36,500 lb
Crew number	Four-five
Maximum speed	255 m.p.h.
Service ceiling	22,000 ft
Normal range	1,885 miles
Armament	Eight machine guns; up to 4,000 lb of bombs

Wellington: Comparison of Marks

		IC	II	III	IV
Span	Ft in.	86 2	86 2	86 2	86 2
Length	Ft in.	64 7	64 7	60 10	NA
Height	Ft in.	17 5	17 5	17 5	NA
Weight	Lb	28,500	33,000	29,500	31,600
Speed	m.p.h.	235	247	255	229
at	Ft	15,500	NV	12,500	NV
Ceiling	Ft	18,000	23,500	19,000	21,250
Range	Miles	2,550	2,220	2,200	2,180

		V	VI	VIII	X
Span	Ft in.	98 2	86 2	86 2	86 2
Length	Ft in.	NA	61 9	64 7	64 7
Height	Ft in.	NA	17 8	17 8	17 8
Weight	Lb	32,000	30,450	30,000	36,500
Speed	m.p.h.	292	300	235	255
at	Ft	NV	NV	NV	NV
Ceiling	Ft	36,800	38,500	19,000	22,000
Range	Miles	2,250	2,275	2,550	1,885

		XI	XII	XIII	XIV
Span	Ft in.	86 2	86 2	86 2	86 2
Length	Ft in.	60 10	NV	64 7	NV
Height	Ft in.	17 0	NV	17 8	NV
Weight	Lb	29,500	36,500	31,000	31,000
Speed	m.p.h.	255	256	250	250
at	Ft	NV	NV	NV	NV
Ceiling	Ft	19,000	18,500	16,000	16,000
Range	Miles	2,020	1,810	1,760	1,760

The Wellington was the leading twin-engine medium bomber of the R.A.F. During the first half of the war it was virtually the narrative of Bomber Command. The outstanding constructional and visual feature of the Wellington was its unique geodetic structure, which made it capable of taking incredible punishment and yet getting back to base. The Wellington was already with the R.A.F. in 1939 – deliveries arriving at the same sort of period as its fighter counterparts, the Hurricane and Spitfire. From September 1939, in fact, it continued to see service as a bomber for five and a half years. No aeroplane could have been in action sooner. The day after war broke out, Wellingtons made a raid against enemy warships at anchor in Wilhelmshafen. The Wellington I was powered by two 1,000 h.p. Bristol Pegasus XVIII engines. It became a night-bomber early in the war, taking the main strain of the R.A.F. commitment in this sphere, until the Lancaster and later arrivals relieved it. One of its other earlier duties was to locate and destroy German magnetic mines. This was achieved through activating the mines by means of flying overhead with a gigantic degaussing circle of metal fitted to the Wellington. The bomb load of the aeroplane at this stage was some 4,500 lb, and to the Wellington went the record of carrying and dropping the 4,000 lb blockbuster bomb before any other aircraft. The Wellington II had 1,145 h.p. Rolls Royce Merlin X engines; the III had 1,375 h.p. Bristol Hercules III or 1,500 h.p. Hercules XI engines; the IV was powered by 1,200 h.p. Pratt and Whitney Twin Wasps. The next significant version was the VIII long-range general reconnaissance-bomber with Coastal Command. This mark was the one fitted to carry two 18 in. torpedoes, depth charges or mines. The last and most important Wellington was the X. This was powered by twin Bristol Hercules VI or XVI engines and served as a medium bomber resembling the III, apart from the engines. The actual production figure for the X was 3,804, manufactured from 1943-45. The Wellington flew from bases in Britain, the Middle East, North Africa, Italy and India. Total production of all marks ran to 11,461 – or even more according to some sources. Just as its first raid had been twenty-four hours after the war started, so its last was only a matter of weeks before VE-Day. This was a sortie against the northern Italian town of Treviso. The Wellington XI was a torpedo-bomber edition of X, while the XII, XIII and XIV were all reconnaissance-bombers; the XV and XVI were transport versions of the bomber; and the XVII and XVIII were trainers.

Illustration in colour section

On 7 July 1941, Sergeant J. Ward was awarded the V.C. for a Wellington attack on Munster. An Me 110 hit the bomber repeatedly, setting fire to the starboard engine and wing. They were over the coast of the Zuider Zee and did not want to crash or bale out over Europe or the sea. So while the pilot tried to fly the whining, protesting Wellington, Ward clambered out of the cockpit and along the blazing wing of the shattered bomber. It was worse than being in a raging gale. Somehow in the darkness, he managed to stop the fire from spreading and encroaching beyond the area of the petrol pipe. Eventually it burned itself out, he got back into the Wellington, and they all got home. An incredible feat.

Whitley (Armstrong Whitworth)

Mk V

Engines	Two 1,145 h.p. Rolls Royce Merlin X inlines
Span	84 ft
Length	70 ft 6 ins
Height	15 ft
Weight empty	19,350 lb
Weight loaded	33,500 lb
Crew number	Five
Maximum speed	230 m.p.h. at 16,400 ft
Service ceiling	26,000 ft
Normal range	1,500 miles
Armament	Five .303 machine guns; up to 7,000 lb of bombs

Whitley: Comparison of Marks

		I	II	III
Span	Ft in.	84 0	84 0	84 0
Length	Ft in.	69 3	69 3	69 3
Height	Ft in.	15 0	15 0	15 0
Weight	Lb	21,660	22,990	22,990
Speed	m.p.h.	183	209	209
at	Ft	16,400	16,400	16,400
Ceiling	Ft	19,200	23,000	23,000
Range	Miles	1,250	1,315	1,315

		IV	V	VII
Span	Ft in.	84 0	84 0	84 0
Length	Ft in.	69 3	70 6	70 6
Height	Ft in.	15 0	15 0	15 0
Weight	Lb	25,900	33,500	33950
Speed	m.p.h.	244	230	215
at	Ft	16,400	16,400	16,400
Ceiling	Ft	NV	26,000	20,000
Range	Miles	1,250	1,500	2,300

The Whitley was the first two-engine, so-called 'heavy' bomber to be manufactured in quantity for the Royal Air Force. It began to be delivered in 1937. When war broke out, the Whitley was one of the leading British bombers – with a maximum load of 7,000 lb of bombs – and executed all that was required of it in those early days. Right from September 1939, the Whitley was flying on operations; at that time it was the leaflet raids on the enemy. The Whitley was the first R.A.F. bomber to fly over the German capital. It made the first bombing attack on Germany in May 1940, and on Italy the following month. It dropped paratroops over southern

Italy in February 1941 during a little-remembered operation. The Whitley was withdrawn from front-line service with Bomber Command in 1942 and served with Coastal Command until early 1943. Training and reconnaissance were still further roles. The Whitley I was powered by a pair of Armstrong Siddeley Tiger IX engines of 795 h.p. The Whitley II had Tiger VIII engines of 845 h.p. The Whitley III differed from all other variants being fitted with a retractable 'dustbin turret'. The Whitley IV had two Rolls Royce Merlin IV engines of 1,030 h.p., and the Whitley IVA had Merlin Xs at 1,075 h.p. The Whitley V also had the same Merlins and was delivered to the R.A.F. as early as August 1939. It was the VII that represented the Coastal Command Whitley, flown for reconnaissance, convoy protection, and anti-U-boat purposes, and bearing long-range radar equipment.

Illustration in colour section

Wildcat (Grumman)

F4F-3

Engine	One 1,200 h.p. Pratt and Whitney Twin Wasp radial
Span	38 ft
Length	28 ft 9 ins
Height	11 ft 11 ins
Weight empty	5,238 lb
Weight loaded	7,065 lb
Crew number	One
Maximum speed	331 m.p.h. at 21,300 ft
Service ceiling	37,000 ft
Normal ra ge	860 miles
Armament	Four .50 machine guns; two 100 lb bombs, optional

The Wildcat was an American fighter designed and developed for operation from aircraft-carriers of the U.S. Navy. The first production aeroplane flew early in 1940. A French order for modified Wildcats was placed about the same time, but before any aircraft could reach their destination France fell – and so Britain took over the order. At this stage, the Wildcats for the British Fleet Air Arm were renamed Martlets. Reaching the Royal Navy at the height of the Battle of Britain, they went straight into service by October. This Martlet I version was powered by a 1,200 h.p. Wright Cyclone engine. The Martlet II succeeded it in the following year, powered by a 1,200 h.p. Pratt and Whitney Twin Wasp radial engine. These incorporated the modification of folding wings for compact carrier stowage. Marks III, IV, V

and VI followed in quantity. Literally thousands of Wildcats/Martlets were manufactured, either for American or British naval forces. In true bureaucratic fashion, the British version resumed the original American christening of Wildcat in 1944! The Martlet III had fixed wings as on Martlet I. The Wildcat suffered from some weight problems derived from additional equipment. Despite this, however, it continued as a prime power among Fleet Air Arm fighters throughout the war, flying in all the familiar naval-air roles in the Mediterranean, and also playing a part in the Battle of the Atlantic. Production continued until the very month of total victory – August 1945. This under-rated fighter and fighter-bomber served for nearly five years; perhaps its fame was rather restricted because it was at sea so much. The Hellcat was a more powerful development of the Wildcat, made by the same manufacturers. The Fleet Air Arm received some 250 F Mk I Hellcats under Lend-Lease, and later on it received F Mk II and NF Mk IIs to a total of one thousand. Speeds were 375 m.p.h. for the Hellcat I and 366 m.p.h. for the II.

Illustration in colour section

York (Avro)

Mk I

Engines	Four 1,620 h.p. Rolls Royce Merlin T24 or 502
Span	102 ft
Length	78 ft 6 ins
Height	16 ft 6 ins
Weight empty	42,040 lb
Weight loaded	68,000 lb
Crew number	Five
Maximum speed	298 m.p.h.
Service ceiling	26,000 ft
Maximum range	2,700 miles
Armament	NV

The York was a four-engine transport powered by 1,620 h.p. Rolls Royce Merlin T24 engine or Merlin 502. Its appearance featured the high-set cantilever monoplane wing and an approximately rectangular cross-section of its main fuselage. The crew numbered four or five and the York could carry up to fifty or even more passengers. The few in service during the war itself flew as transports for V.I.P.s, and it was not until well into 1945 that complete York squadrons began to be formed and flown. It had a good speed performance of 298 m.p.h. and top range of 2,700 miles. The York did not really come into its own till post-war years.

Above: York transport powered by four Rolls-Royce Merlin XX engines

IN ACTION

The RAF during the Second World War

Aircraft of the Royal Air Force served all over the world during the Second World War. The following account cannot cover all the numerous types of action in which they were involved, but they have been selected to provide an illuminating picture of what fighting in these aeroplanes was really like. The accounts cover great air battles, individual feats of heroism, aeroplane versus aeroplane and aeroplane versus ship encounters, ground attacks, special missions, and so on. They include stories not only of aeroplanes of British manufacture, but also of American aeroplanes in British service. They are a tribute to the aircraft themselves and to the men who flew them.

Bridge-busting

Blenheim, Battle and Hurricane

On 10 May 1940 German forces smashed into the Low Countries. So sudden was the Allied withdrawal from their prepared positions along the Meuse that they did not have time to blow up the Maastricht bridge as they had all the others on this reach of the river. Now the bridge was to become a threat to the retreating armies as the Germans built up a powerful force in the bridge area. Once across, the Germans would be in a position to cut the Allied front in two.

The order went out to R.A.F. bomber squadrons stationed in France to destroy the bridge, but the Germans had defended their gain strongly. Ground guns kept up a barrage of fire against the attacking aircraft, and enemy fighters maintained constant patrols. Yet in spite of these defences the R.A.F. made eight separate attacks on 10 and 11 May. Pinpoint bombing, at that stage of the war and in those conditions, however, was out of the question. None of the eight sorties succeeded.

To some extent, the whole operation in Europe depended on that one bridge, yet the umbrella of fighter cover, coupled with the ground guns, made any further attacks almost impossible. Such was the situation on 12 May, only two days after the start of the attack on the Low Countries.

On that day two separate attacks were made by two separate squadrons. First, a squadron of Blenheims delivered an attack from 3,000 feet in the face of fierce anti-aircraft fire. Their leader described it afterwards not only as the heaviest he had ever encountered but also as the heaviest he could have imagined. On approaching the target, the squadron broke formation in order to run in from several directions, but as they were bombing the leader spotted enemy fighters and immediately called on his squadron to regain formation. They did so at once and faced the fighters, which were driven off by concerted fire. Of the twelve Blenheims, eight returned to their base, and every one of them had been hit.

That same day, the commanding officer of No. 12 Squadron stationed at Amifontaine assembled his pilots and called for volunteers to attack Maastricht. Every pilot stepped forward, but as

only five Battles were wanted the pilots scribbled their names on slips of paper and the five crews were chosen by ballot.

The five bombers were escorted by a fighter force of Hurricanes, and leading the five was the Battle piloted by Flying Officer Donald Garland. Still a few weeks off his twenty-second birthday, Garland had been promoted from pilot officer only three months earlier. With him in the single-engine Fairey Battle flew Sergeant Thomas Gray, an observer with more than ten years' service since his enlistment in 1929 as an apprentice.

While the Battles flew straight for Maastricht, the Hurricanes swept the sky to ward off any opposition from enemy fighters. But as the bombers could not hope to effect any surprise, they were bound to meet heavy anti-aircraft fire, against which the Hurricanes would be powerless. The way back – if there were one – would have to be through fast fighter formations of the Luftwaffe.

As the bridge, which spanned a section of the Meuse known as the Albert Canal, moved into sight through a haze of early ack-ack bursts, enemy fighters put in their first appearance. The Hurricanes kept these clear of the five Battles, but of course could not prevent the ground guns from getting an accurate range on the bombers, which had to fly through a blizzard of shrapnel. German machine gun posts, too, joined the heavier fire.

Dive-bombing

Lashed by flak, the leading Battle flew on into the fire, machine gun bullets embedding themselves in the fuselage and the whole bomber rocking from the blast of a near miss. Through the smoke Garland glimpsed German lorries on the bridge as he pushed his stick down directly towards the bridge, diving straight through twin bursts of fire and loosing his bomb-load. In spite of the opposition he delivered his dive-bombing attack from the lowest possible altitude and the other four Battles followed.

A plume of water beside one of the supports signalled a very close thing. A lorry belched oil fumes about a third of the way across the bridge, halting the following traffic. Not that it could have continued anyway, for one of the bombs scored a direct hit, right in the centre of the bridge's roadway. The surface crumbled away and struts collapsed. The whole bridge area became a mass of flames obscuring the vision of the Hurricane pilots high above. Yet, as it cleared a little, they could be sure of one thing: the bridge was blown. Later reconnaissance confirmed that one end of the bridge had been demolished and the structure temporarily put out of action.

'Bombs gone', Garland and the other pilots pushed up their sticks again. Now they had to get away from Maastricht. Garland had flown them there; Gray had navigated. The official account was to refer to Gray's 'coolness and resource'. But on the way out the inevitable happened. Enemy fighters broke through the screen of Hurricanes to attack the already scarred Battles. Exactly what happened no one will ever know, but as a result of either ground or air attack four of the five bombers crashed. Garland and Gray, as leaders, attracted most enemy attention, so it was inevitable they would be hit and killed – as they were. One plane plunged into the river; another ploughed furrows in the fields. Only one much damaged Battle returned home.

After Maastricht

Heroic as the action had been, though, it did not stop the enemy advance. Two days later the Germans crossed the Meuse at two places, one near Sedan – famous from the First World War.

At first it seemed possible to destroy the bridges they were using. Six Battles made the first attack at about 5 a.m. All returned, the pilot of one being wounded. Shortly after 7.30 a.m., four more Battles renewed attacks and hits were claimed on a pontoon bridge near Sedan. All four returned safely. However, the situation deteriorated, and by two o'clock a much larger force of bombers was standing by to attack this and four other bridges between Mouzon and Sedan. Sixty-seven Battles took off soon after three o'clock; thirty-two returned. The rest had fallen to intense anti-aircraft fire and the German fighters. Two pontoon bridges were destroyed and another damaged, and two permanent bridges received direct hits.

During the days that followed, six crews of the Battles filtered back to their base, among them a pilot, wounded in two places, who succeeded in swimming the Meuse. An observer and an air gunner had tended their wounded pilot for more than twenty-four hours, leaving him only when he died. They also crossed the Meuse to safety. But the bravery of the bomber crews was rendered of little account. The bridges were broken; so too were the French. The Germans had found other avenues for their advance.

Crashed Seven Times

Spitfire

When the New Zealand pilot Al Deere sat in a Spitfire for the first time in 1940 he said: 'At first the speed amazed me. I was frightened out of my life and absolutely scared to do other than fly straight and level. This soon wore off, and before long Spitfires were being aerobated to the utmost. A Spitfire is the most beautiful and easy aircraft to fly and has no tricks or peculiarities normally attributable to high-speed fighters.' Nevertheless, Deere's high opinions of the aircraft did not prevent him getting into trouble seven times during the war – and surviving.

The first time Deere was shot down caused him little trouble – so will not be counted. The next occurred only two days later. During a protective patrol over the Dunkirk evacuation, his Spitfire was hit by the tail gunner of a Dornier, causing the glycol to start leaking from the aeroplane. Despite this, Deere returned the Dornier's fire for as long as he could see ahead, but his aircraft was so disabled that there was nothing for him to do but crash-land somewhere on the beach. He managed this, quite an achievement in the circumstances, but the impact knocked him out. Coming round a minute or two later and immediately aware of the engine smoking, he ripped off his straps, got clear of the cockpit, and sat down on the beach. At that moment he could only curse his bad luck, rather than appreciate how lucky he was to be alive. He had commanded his flight for barely one hour before being shot down, for the second time in three days.

After twelve days of continuous action around and over Dunkirk, Deere and his squadron were rested. They returned to active service in the middle of June. In the early days of July, going out to intercept enemy raiders leaving Calais, Deere took his flight up to 8,000 feet to patrol over Deal, where they encountered a silver seaplane, twelve Me 109s flying at about 1,000 feet, and another five Messerschmitts well behind at 6,000 feet. Deere led a section of Spitfires to attack the five Messerschmitts, and, having shot down one of them, saw another coming up on his tail. Doing a steep turn to meet the enemy head-on, he fired at the same time as the German.

He described the rest of the action himself:

'We were dead head-on and he was right in my sights. I don't remember whether I thought about avoiding a collision by breaking away, but things seemed to happen so suddenly. The first awakening was a large nose looming up in front of me. There was a terrific and horrible thud and then my aircraft began to vibrate so violently that I thought my engine must surely shake itself off the bearers. Black smoke poured into the cockpit and flames appeared from the engine. I reached to open the hood in order to bale out, only to discover that his propeller had struck the front of my windscreen and the whole fixture was so twisted I could not move the hood.

I could not see for smoke, but managed to ascertain that I was headed inland. Nearly blinded and choked I succeeded in keeping the air speed at about 100 miles an hour. The engine had now seized and I was just waiting to hit the ground. Suddenly there was a terrific jerk, and I was tossed left then right and finally pitched forward on my straps, which fortunately held fast. I seemed to plough through all sorts of things and then stop.

The remains of my ammunition were going off in a series of pops and the flames were getting very near the cockpit. I frantically broke open the hood and, undoing my harness, ran to a safe distance. My eyebrows were singed, both my knees were bruised, but otherwise I was uninjured. The Spitfire was blazing furiously in the middle of a cornfield and had left a trail of broken posts and pieces of wing, plus the complete tail unit, extending for 200 yards.'

The next day, Deere was back on patrol.

Battle of Britain

The remainder of Deere's escapes overlap into the Battle of Britain. On 10 August, leading his Spitfire squadron against 100 Me 109s, he caught a German so intent on a flaming Hurricane that he failed to see the Spitfire pilot, who blew him to bits in the air. But a minute or two later, Deere, himself intent on another victim, was caught the same way and forced to land. That was his fourth escape.

His fifth escape followed an attack by No. 54 Squadron on a formation of 200 bombers, an encounter in which Deere added to his mounting score. After watching three German bombers floating down in flames, Deere chased two enemy fighters right across the Channel and was surprised to find himself over Calais Marck aerodrome. As he turned, five Me 109s dived on top of him. He takes up the story:

'Bullets seemed to be coming from everywhere and pieces were flying off my aircraft. My instrument panel was shattered, my eye was bleeding from a splinter, my watch had been shot clean off my wrist by an incendiary bullet which left a nice diagonal burn across my wrist and it seemed only a matter of moments before the end.

Never did it take so long to get across thirty miles of sea and never had my aircraft gone so slowly. My good old Merlin engine carried me safely across, however, and had just reached Folkestone when my pursuers broke off the engagement. None too soon. Two minutes later my engine – I was now at 800 feet – burst into flames. Desperately I tore my straps off, pulled back the hood and prepared to bail out. I was still doing about 300 miles an hour, so I pulled the stick back to get a bit more height. At about 1,500 feet I turned my back and pushed the stick hard forward. I shot out a few feet and somehow became caught up by the bottom of my parachute. I twisted and turned, but wasn't able to get either in or out. The nose had now dropped below the horizontal and was pointing at the ground, which appeared to be rushing up at a terrific speed. Suddenly I was blown along the side of the fuselage, hitting my wrist a nasty smack on the tail. Then I was clear. I made a desperate grasp at the ripcord and with a jolt the parachute opened. None too soon. I hadn't time to breathe a sigh of relief before I landed with a mighty thud in a plantation of thick shrubs.'

Those shrubs probably saved his life. As he lay there, shaken but unharmed, his Spitfire went up in flames in the next field. The following day he was on duty with a strapped-up wrist as evidence of his adventure. And two days later he had just shot down an enemy when his own Spitfire was disabled and he had to make a forced landing.

Abandon aircraft

A few days after that in a fight that started at 34,000 feet, he was diving after a plane he had shot down when he found himself in the middle of another formation of Messerschmitts flying at 28,000 feet. One of the enemy promptly shot away his rudder controls.

As he dived away, his engine began to smoke,

which indicated that the aircraft would probably go up in flames if he made a crash-landing, so he decided to bail out. Controlling the Spitfire by using the ailerons until he was down to 10,000 feet, he prepared to abandon his aircraft. The vivid memory of how he was caught on the previous occasion led him to adopt another method this time, so he stalled the burning Spitfire and took a header over the side as if he was diving off a springboard into a swimming pool. Directly he saw the tail of his aircraft overhead he pulled his ripcord and floated gently down, taking the opportunity of practising side-slipping by working the lines of his parachute. It was as well that he practised, for he was obliged to side-slip to miss a farmhouse. He landed right in the middle of a heavily laden plum tree.

So much for the sixth escape. As a change from being shot down, Deere was next nearly killed on the ground. He had just made two sorties, on the day following the plum tree episode, and was about to take off for a third when a formation of Heinkels bombed the aerodrome. As he opened his throttle, a bomb fell right in front of him. He seemed to be flung miles in the air, then he felt himself careering along the ground upside down with his head scraping over the earth and squeezing him into a ball in the cockpit. He thought it was the end for him, but the aircraft stopped at last and he was still alive.

Every moment he thought the flames would creep in on him, but Pilot Officer E. Edsall managed to get the door off and haul him out.

'I was balanced on my head, so there was no danger of breaking my neck when I released my Sutton harness,' Deere explained humorously. His scalp was bleeding and caked with earth and he was very dazed, but otherwise he was unharmed.

'When I saw the wreckage of my aircraft afterwards I just didn't believe I had come out alive. The engine had been blown completely off, the starboard wing was some hundreds of yards away, the tail unit was nowhere to be seen and there was a furrow about 100 yards in length where I had ploughed along upside down. I think the engine being blown up saved me from fire, as there was a considerable amount of petrol in the tank.'

Next day, with concussion and a sore head, and although grounded by the medical officer, Deere shot down a Dornier into the Thames. Altogether, Squadron Leader Alan C. Deere, D.F.C. and bar, destroyed seventeen enemy aircraft.

The seventh of his extraordinary escapes came when he was teaching tactics to a pupil pilot. His pupil misjudged the distances between their two Spitfires and flew right into Deere's aircraft, cutting it in two. Deere was so caught up among the wreckage that he found it impossible to bail out, and while struggling to disentangle himself he dropped several thousand feet.

Eventually he broke free, but his parachute harness was half torn off and the ripcord handle was dangling out of his reach six feet below. In vain he tried to get at it. As the earth rushed up at him, he closed his eyes and waited, but a mighty jerk on his shoulders made him open them again. The parachute had functioned of its own accord. Yet when the parachute was examined, it was found that the ripcord pin had never been pulled.

Night Flying

Beaufighter, Hurricane and Mosquito

After fighting with distinction in the Battle of Britain, John Cunningham turned to night flying as the need for night-fighters rose urgently when the Battle of Britain merged into the blitz on London and other British cities. Just how the blitz was beaten can be illustrated through the experiences of 'Cat's Eyes' Cunningham. Cunningham was called up a matter of days before war broke out, his first posting being 604 Squadron, which he later commanded. His night-fighting career began in the early winter months of 1940, and his first success was on 19 November, when he destroyed a Ju 88 over the east Midlands.

By the beginning of the new year, Britain's winter weather, coupled with better defences in anti-aircraft guns, barrage balloons and night-fighters, resulted in a change of enemy plans. Instead of concentrating a large number of bombers in space and time over a target, Goering switched to smaller groups which were scheduled to reach their targets at successive periods in order to prolong the raids. The barrage balloons and the guns kept the bombers high, while the night-fighters tackled them eagerly.

By spring 1941, Cunningham had became both

Air against Sea

Left: Beaufighters in rocket attack on German minesweepers, 1944. The photo was taken looking backwards from a Beaufighter. Below left: Attack on shipping in Norwegian harbour. Mosquito pulling out after its rockets had exploded. Below: Depth-charge dropped by Sunderland on German U-boat, 1944. Bottom: Bombs from low-flying Mosquitos straddle enemy shipping at the mouth of the Gironde, France

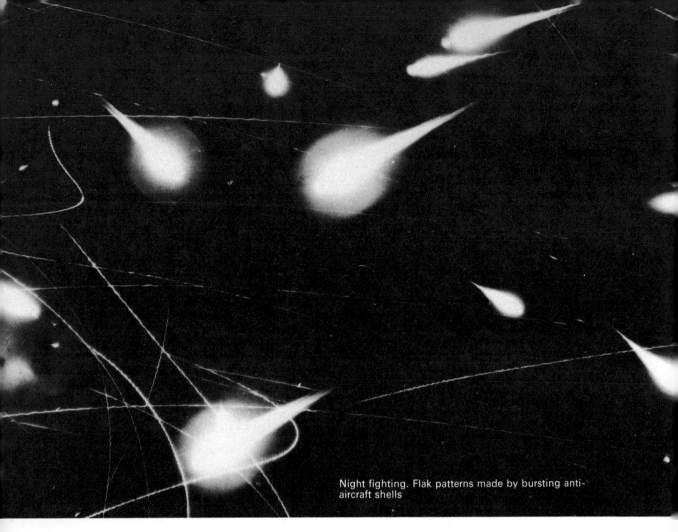

Night fighting. Flak patterns made by bursting anti-aircraft shells

busy and successful. Night flying was a different, alien world where impressions were muted. The stars and moon provided his only light from above, and below the cities were blacked out completely unless an occasional fire from enemy bombs or incendiaries broke the darkness. Yet Cunningham had to know exactly where he was all the time. A 24-year-old pilot with less than two years' experience behind him, he adapted himself and grew accustomed to this unlit universe. When an enemy raid was on, of course, he could see the stabs of searchlights hunting out the bombers, and the curving tracer-sprays or shell-bursts far below. Or perhaps a pattern of coloured lights would dot the earth, denoting an airfield. Cunningham learned to absorb all these distant images instinctively and to react to them rationally yet rapidly.

He flew in a dim mixture of darkness and stellar sheen, at a speed approaching twice that of the enemy bombers, and he learned to recognize the ghostly glow of an aircraft on a bombing mission. His main job then was to keep it in range long enough to make an attack. It hardly needs stressing how very difficult the art of night-fighting was, but Cunningham mastered all its hazards to become the greatest night-fighter ace of all. He hated being referred to by his nickname of 'Cat's Eyes' though.

He was airborne in a Bristol Beaufighter on the night of 11–12 April 1941, when base radio notified him of the approximate details of enemy bombers. Working within the network of the coastal ground control interception stations, he continued to be guided by base radio towards the enemy until the aircraft's own radar navigation picked them up on the small screen. With him as usual on this flight as A.I. operator was Sergeant C. F. 'Jimmy' Rawnsley.

This was what happened on that particular patrol, as told in the tense, technical style of the report:

'Put on to north-bound raid 13,000 feet. Final vector 360 degrees and buster [full speed].

Told to flash [to operate A.I.] but no contact received. G.C.I. station then told us to alter course to 350 degrees and height 11,000 feet. While going from 13,000 to 11,000 a blip [flash of light in A.I. set] was picked up at max. range ahead. On operator's instructions I closed in and obtained a visual at 2,500 feet range [checked on A.I. set] and about 30 degrees up.

Identified E/A [enemy aircraft] as He 111 which was flying just beneath cloud layer and occasionally going through wisps which allowed me to get within 80 yards of E/A and about 20 to 30 feet beneath before opening fire. Immediately there was a big white flash in the fuselage centre section and black pieces flew off the fuselage. E/A went into a vertical dive to the right, and about half a minute later the sky all around was lit up by an enormous orange flash and glow. Bits of E/A were seen to be burning on the ground.

I estimated my position to be about Shaftesbury but called Harlequin and asked for a fix so that my exact position could be checked.

One He 111 destroyed. Rounds fired 64.'

Toy town below

Cunningham made it sound easy. Flying by day in cloud was hard enough. Doing this at night was immeasurably more so. As well as good eyesight, the pilot had to possess other vital qualities for success or survival. The night-fighter pilots used to spend a short time before operations in dimly lit rooms, wearing dark glasses.

Here now is how Cunningham described one of his many operations.

'Try to imagine the moonlit sky, with a white background of snow nearly six miles below. Somewhere near the centre of a toy town, a tiny place is burning. Several enemy bombers have come over, but only one fire has gained hold. After all the excitement of my combats, I can still see that amazing picture of London clearly in my mind.

It was indeed the kind of night that we fly-by-nights pray for. I had been up about three-quarters of an hour before I found an enemy aircraft, having searched all round the sky when I suddenly saw him ahead of me. I pulled the boost control to get the highest possible speed and catch him up. I felt my Hurricane vibrate all over as she responded and gave maximum power.

I manoeuvred into position where I could see the enemy clearly with the least chance of his seeing me. As I caught him up I recognized him – a Dornier 'Flying Pencil'. Before I spotted him I had been almost petrified with the cold. I was beginning to wonder if I should ever be able to feel my hands, feet or limbs again. But the excitement warmed me up.

He was now nearly within range and was climbing to 30,000 feet. I knew the big moment had come. I daren't take my eyes off him, but just to make sure that everything was all right I took a frantic glance round the 'office' – that's what we call the cockpit – and checked everything. Then I began to close in on the Dornier and found I was travelling much too fast. I throttled back and slowed up just in time. We were frighteningly close. Then I swung up, took aim, and fired my eight guns. Almost at once I saw little flashes of fire dancing along the fuselage and centre section. My bullets had found their mark.

I closed in again, when suddenly the bomber reared up in front of me. It was all I could do to avoid crashing into him. I heaved at the controls to prevent a collision, and in doing so I lost sight of him. I wondered if he was playing pussy and intending to jink away, come up on the other side and take a crack at me, or whether he was hard hit. The next moment I saw him going down below me with a smoke trail pouring out.

Some of you may have seen that smoke trail. I felt a bit disappointed, because it looked as if my first shots had not been as effective as they appeared. Again I pulled the boost control and went down after him as fast as I knew how. I dived from 30,000 feet at such a speed that the bottom panel of the aircraft cracked, and as my ears were not used to such sudden changes of pressure I nearly lost the use of one of my drums. But there was no time to think of these things. I had to get that bomber. Then as I came nearer I saw he was on fire. Little flames were flickering around his fuselage and wings. Just as I closed in again he jinked away in a steep climbing turn.

I was going too fast again, so I pulled the stick back and went up after him in a screaming left-hand climbing turn. When he got to the top of his climb I was almost on him. I took sight very carefully and gave the button a quick squeeze. Once more I saw little dancing lights on his fuselage, but almost simultaneously they were swallowed in a burst of flames. I saw him twist gently earthwards and there was a spurt of fire as he touched the earth. He blew up and set a copse blazing.

I circled down to see if any of the crew had got out, and then I suddenly remembered the London balloon barrage, so I climbed up and set course for home.

I had time now to think about the action. My windscreen was covered with oil, which made flying uncomfortable and I had a nasty feeling that I might have lost bits of my aircraft. I remembered seeing bits of Jerry flying past me. There were several good-sized holes in the fabric, which could have been caused only by hefty lumps of Dornier. Also the engine seemed to be running a bit roughly, but that turned out to be my imagination. Anyway, I soon landed, reported what had happened, had some refreshment and then up in the air once more, southward ho for London.

Soon after, I was at 17,000 feet. It's a bit warmer there than 30,000. I slowed down and searched the sky. The next thing I knew a Heinkel was sitting right on my tail. I was certain he had seen me, and wondered how long he had been trailing me. I opened my throttle, got round on his tail and crept up. When I was about 400 yards away he opened fire – and missed. I checked my gadgets, then I closed up and snaked about so as to give him as difficult a target as possible. I got into a firing position, gave a quick burst of my guns and broke away.

I came up again, and it looked as if my shots had had no effect. Before I could fire a second time, I saw his tracer bullets whizzing past me. I fired back and I knew at once that I had struck home. I saw a parachute open up on the port wing. One of the crew was bailing out. He was quickly followed by another. The round white domes of the parachutes looked lovely in the moonlight.

It was obvious now that the pilot would never get his aircraft home and I, for my part, wanted this second machine to be a 'certainty' and not a 'probable'. So I gave another quick burst of my guns. Then to fool him I attacked from different angles. There was no doubt now that he was going down. White smoke was coming from one engine, but he was not yet on fire. I delivered seven more attacks, spending all my ammunition. Both his engines smoked as he got lower and lower. I followed him down a long way and as he flew over a dark patch of water I lost sight of him.

But I knew he had come down, and where he had come down – it was all confirmed later – and

I returned to my base ready to tackle another one. But they told me all the Jerries had gone home. "Not all,' I said. 'Two of them are here . . . for keeps".'

Close call

One of Cunningham's closest escapes came in August 1941. Shortly after joining a new squadron, he took off in a Beaufighter on a night interception over East Anglia. It was, in fact, his first operational flight with his new squadron, and he marked it by shooting down a Heinkel. But an hour or so later, on the same patrol, he spotted another aircraft. After one long-range burst he found that his aircraft was overshooting his quarry and turned away for another attack. As he did so the enemy opened fire on him, piercing the petrol pipe to the port engine. Not surprisingly, the engine gave out, but Cunningham managed to get back to base and land with just his starboard engine.

So it went on. Cunningham and Rawnsley gathered decorations regularly, and became well established as the leading night-fighter team. The pilot described his sixteenth victory like this.

'There was nothing left but a hole in the ground after I went to inspect the wreckage. The combat was over in a matter of minutes. I got on his tail, gave him less than a half-second burst and he caught fire. He crashed not far from my airfield.

The German pilot who is in hospital was thrown out as the Fw began to break up. He had the presence of mind to pull his ripcord. When I landed they told me he had been taken to hospital suffering from burns.'

Cunningham disposed of one adversary without using a single bullet. After a hard tussle, in which he had used up all his ammunition, he decided to dive on the enemy aircraft, a move that so staggered his enemy that he too dived to try to evade Cunningham. The enemy, however, left it too late to straighten up again and crashed.

Gradually, ground and air radar advanced, and by New Year's Day 1944 Cunningham's successes had a certain inevitability about them. The only change was that he now flew a Mosquito. At one minute past midnight on 2 January, Cunningham shot down a fast enemy bomber attempting to raid Britain, bringing his score to nineteen. Later he said:

'We had a bit of a chase after this one – in fact

we went right across the Channel to the French coast. My observer spotted it as an Me 410. It sped off homewards, taking evasive action all the time. However, our Mosquito was faster, and when I came within 250 yards, right behind it, I gave it a short burst.

There was an explosion and considerable flame. The bomber dived away sharply and for a moment I lost sight of it. I looked down and realized that I was over the French coast, somewhere near Le Touquet. Next moment I saw the Hun again, this time exploding in a great flash on the ground, and a big orange glow was my last sight of it.'

Needless to say, the observer he referred to was still Jimmy Rawnsley.

The glow was later reported to have been seen by a Royal Observer post on the English side of the Channel.

Gradually the night-bomber blitz was beaten. The fighter pilots grew more and more experienced, and with the aid of radar to detect enemy bombers before they crossed the coast, the night-fighters could be ready and waiting. Eventually, the enemy turned to the V.1s and V.2s, but these too were mastered.

John Cunningham continued in the R.A.F. until the war was won, and then he rejoined de Havillands. One day in 1948, he took a de Havilland Vampire fighter, with a Ghost jet engine, up to a world record altitude of nearly 60,000 feet: twice the height of those nights when he fought and beat the bombers.

Hunting the Bismarck

Whitley, Hudson, Maryland, Sunderland, Catalina, Swordfish and Fulmar

'I give you the hunter's toast: good hunting and a good bag.' With these words Admiral Lutjens ended his speech to the ship's company of the *Bismarck*. They were heard throughout the vessel; those who could not be on deck listened to them through the loudspeakers situated in various parts of the battleship.

The time was a few minutes past noon on Monday, 19 May 1941. That evening the *Bismarck* weighed anchor and put to sea, taking a northerly course from Kiel Bay. It was the intention of

Admiral Lutjens to raid commerce in the Atlantic, just as he had done earlier in the year, flying his flag in the *Gneisenau*, which together with the *Scharnhorst* had sunk twenty-two British and Allied ships, including the *Jervis Bay*. The *Gneisenau* and *Scharnhorst* were now in Brest and had already suffered damage from the attack made on them by aircraft of Bomber and Coastal Commands. If Germany was to obtain a decision in the Battle of the Atlantic, other units of her navy had to be sent to sea, and the *Bismarck* and the *Prinz Eugen* were chosen. For the *Bismarck* it was her first and last voyage.

She formed the main unit of a squadron made up of the 8-inch cruiser *Prinz Eugen*, two destroyers and two mine-bumpers. After passing through the Great Belt, the squadron moved up the coast of occupied Norway and, on the morning of 21 May, entered a fiord near Bergen, where it anchored. There had been little sleep on board that night, for an air raid alarm had kept the crews at action stations until half past eight in the morning. And in the early afternoon there was another alarm that lasted a quarter of an hour. A little before dusk the squadron put to sea again.

That day, an aircraft of Coastal Command, in the course of a reconnaissance of the Norwegian coast, had flown as far north as Bergen, where, reconnoitring the approaches to the port, the pilot had discovered two warships, one of large size, at anchor in a small fiord. On his return he made a cautious report of what he had seen to one of the station intelligence officers. While they were talking the prints of the photographs the pilot had taken were brought in, and the intelligence officer saw that what the pilot surmised was indeed the truth. He spoke immediately with Coastal Command headquarters, who ordered the prints be sent direct.

A slight difficulty arose. The only aircraft available to take them to headquarters was that of the pilot who had just finished the patrol. Moreover, it was now evening. Nevertheless, he took off and flew south until, with night fallen, he found himself short of petrol on the outskirts of Nottingham, his home town. Here he landed and roused a friend of his, the owner of a garage and a car. They continued the journey together, driving through the night and the blackout at an average speed of fifty-two m.p.h. The prints were delivered at Coastal Command headquarters in the early hours of the morning, and the Admiralty and the photographic experts confirmed the opinion of the intelligence officer in Scotland. The

Bismarck and the *Prinz Eugen* were out.

Early that same morning the German warships were attacked by six Whitleys and six Lockheed Hudsons of Coastal Command, but the attack was unsuccessful, for the weather was very thick and only two of the aircraft reached the fiord, where they dropped their load of armour-piercing bombs with no observed effect. Throughout that day, 22 May, the weather remained atrocious. Nevertheless, reconnaissance of the Norwegian coast was maintained from first light until dark, every available aircraft of Coastal Command on the east coast of Scotland and the coast of Yorkshire being pressed into service.

They flew at times through a full gale, at times through dense haze and cloud extending downwards to sea level. Hour after hour they plunged into the mist shrouding Bergen harbour and the nearby fiords. It was in vain. No ships were seen, and one pilot expressed the opinion that the enemy was no longer there because 'I collided with nothing though I flew over the harbour at sea-level'.

His conjecture was proved accurate at about 6.30 that evening when the clouds above Bergen lifted for a moment – long enough for a shore-based naval aircraft, a Maryland, to get a clear view that showed there was no warship there.

2,000-mile sorties

Throughout that long day, the *Bismarck* and the *Prinz Eugen* had in fact been steaming steadily northwards, having parted company with their destroyers in the small hours, and at 1 a.m. on 23 May they altered course to pass through the Denmark Strait between Iceland and Greenland. By this time they were fully aware that they had been seen, but they judged that their route offered the best chance of eluding the British fleet now steaming to intercept them.

The weather on 23 May was still very bad – too bad to patrol the Norwegian coast. Sunderland flying boats and Hudsons, however, were able to cover the passages between Iceland and the Faröes and between the Faröes and the Shetlands; the Sunderlands maintaining their patrol in relays from a quarter past six in the morning to a quarter past nine in the evening, the Hudsons from 4 a.m. to 5.15 p.m. The Sunderlands covered more than 2,000 miles in a single sortie; but now the weather was against them as they encountered strong headwinds, fog, rain squalls and heavy cloud, in which severe icing developed. In addition to the Sunderlands, two Catalina flying boats covered the Iceland Channel, beginning their patrol at 1 p.m., but they had to abandon their task when unbroken cloud down to 300 feet, accompanied by unceasing rain, reduced visibility to less than 1,000 yards.

That evening, H.M.S. *Suffolk* sighted the German warships in the Denmark Strait, and soon afterwards a Sunderland and a Hudson from Iceland set off in the long twilight of those far northern latitudes to search for the enemy. The Hudson, unable to find them, returned, but the Sunderland carried on. In the meantime, the *Bismarck* and the *Prinz Eugen* had also been seen by H.M.S. *Norfolk*. The two cruisers shadowed the enemy throughout the night.

Next morning, 24 May, another Hudson took off, and at 5.54 a.m. sighted the *Bismarck* and the *Prinz Eugen* engaged in combat with the *Hood* and the *Prince of Wales*. Low cloud made it impossible to identify the opposing forces with certainty, but it was seen that one of the ships had suffered two direct hits, the second of which had been followed by an explosion.

Meanwhile the Sunderland from Iceland had arrived in the neighbourhood of the *Suffolk*, and on sighting this ship saw at the same time the flash of gunfire well ahead.

'As we closed [says the captain in his report], two columns, each of two ships in line ahead, were seen to be steaming on parallel courses at an estimated range of twelve miles between the columns. Heavy gunfire was being exchanged and the leading ship of the port column was on fire in two places, one fire being at the base of the bridge superstructure and the other farther aft. In spite of these large conflagrations she appeared to be firing at least one turret forward and one aft.'

At first the captain of the Sunderland could not identify the burning ship. He turned towards the starboard column and noticed that the second of its two ships was making a considerable amount of smoke and that oil escaping from her was leaving a broad track on the surface. He went closer, and as he did so the ship on fire in the column to port blew up.

A few seconds later the Sunderland came under heavy anti-aircraft fire, just at the moment its captain was identifying the ships in the starboard column as the *Bismarck* and the *Prinz Eugen*, and he was forced to take immediate cloud cover.

When he emerged into an open patch five minutes later, the damaged ship had almost completely disappeared. He now realized she was British, though he did not learn till later that she was the *Hood*. 'Only part of the bows was showing.' She sank almost at once, and when the Sunderland flew over the spot all that could be seen was an empty raft, painted red, surrounded by wreckage in the midst of a large patch of oil.

Watching the remainder of the action, the captain of the Sunderland saw the *Prince of Wales* turn away under cover of a light smoke-screen and open the range to about fifteen miles. The Sunderland closed on the *Bismarck* to make quite certain of her identity and then, returning to the area of the *Suffolk*, exchanged visual signals with her and learned that the ship sunk was the *Hood*. It was then about 7.15 a.m.

Throughout that day the shadowing of the German ships by the Royal Navy continued. A Catalina of Coastal Command saw them at 12.32 p.m. and remained in contact for two hours, signalling their course and speed to the pursuers at intervals. Coming under anti-aircraft fire, though, the flying boat developed engine trouble that forced it to return to base, and this was the last contact with the enemy made by Coastal Command that day. The *Norfolk* and *Suffolk*, with the *Prince of Wales*, held on, and the *King George V*, in which the commander-in-chief of the Home Fleet was flying his flag, and the aircraft carrier *Victorious* were now rapidly approaching.

Rejoicing – then alarm

On board the *Bismarck* there was much rejoicing, not without good reason. She had damaged the *Prince of Wales*; she had sunk the *Hood*. That evening there was a large extra issue of sausage, chocolate and cigarettes, and Hitler conferred by radio the Knight Insignia of the Iron Cross on the first gunnery officer. True, the speed of the ship had been reduced, for a shell from the *Hood* had partially flooded some of her compartments and had also made it impossible to use the oil fuel in the forward bunkers – it was this leaking oil that had left the broad stain on the sea seen by the Sunderland – but a formidable unit of the British Fleet had been disposed of and another, still more formidable, had been damaged. Surely it was now time to return to the safety of the Norwegian fiords?

Captain Lindemann, in command of the *Bismarck*, thought so; but he was overruled by Admiral Lutjens, who ordered the *Prinz Eugen*

to make for safety alone, while the *Bismarck* held on her course for a French port. Night fell without incident, but soon after midnight torpedo-carrying Swordfish from the *Victorious*, supported by Fulmars, delivered an attack in which a hit was scored on the starboard side. Survivors from the *Bismarck* subsequently spoke with surprise and admiration of the courage displayed by the British pilots. One Swordfish, they said, after being hit, still tried to get into a position from which to release its torpedo, before plunging into the sea. The anti-aircraft fire of the *Bismarck* was tremendous, many of the guns becoming red-hot. British losses in this attack were two Swordfish and two Fulmars, the crews of the Fulmars being saved, though it was put about on board the *Bismarck* that forty-seven British aircraft had been destroyed.

Contact lost

Soon after three o'clock that morning, 25 May, visibility became very bad, and the *Norfolk* and *Suffolk*, which had shadowed the *Bismarck* so tenaciously since sunset on 23 May, at last lost contact with her. When she was last seen, her speed had been reduced to twenty knots. It now seemed to the Admiralty that, in view of the damage she had sustained and her heavy consumption of fuel, she would either double back on her tracks and return to Norway or make for one of the French ports to refuel and refit. Coastal Command did its best to meet both contingencies.

All that afternoon and throughout the night, three Catalinas searched the area. They remained airborne for 19 hours 36 minutes, 20 hours 54 minutes, and 22 hours 21 minutes respectively, yet saw nothing of the enemy, though one of them passed over a warship in the dead of night and was not able to identify it, low cloud making the use of parachute flares impossible.

During 25 May, Hudsons patrolled the Denmark Strait all day in very bad weather, while Sunderlands, with the help of a Catalina and a Hudson, covered the passage between Iceland and the Faröes. None of these aircraft sighted the enemy. Units of the Royal Navy, meanwhile, were taking up fresh positions, with the main body of the Home Fleet steaming at high speed in a south-westerly direction from northern waters and another force, headed by the *Renown*, steaming north-westwards at high speed from Gibraltar. The *Rodney* and the *Ramillies*, on escort duty in the North Atlantic, also proceeded to move in the direction of the enemy.

On board the *Bismarck*, the mood of exaltation was giving way to one of anxiety, which increased to alarm when, shortly before midday, Admiral Lutjens informed the crew that it had proved impossible to shake off the pursuit. Though aircraft and U-boats would be forthcoming as soon as the ship came within their range, an action would almost certainly have to be fought, in which case the best that could be hoped for would be that the *Bismarck* would take some of the Royal Navy to the bottom with her. Yet, as the day wore on and no aircraft were sighted, spirits rose again, especially when they entered a U-boat area.

Dawn broke on 26 May over a heavy sea above which scudded broken clouds. During the morning the weather became somewhat hazy, and at 10.30 a.m. a Catalina appeared above the *Bismarck*. It had taken off from a base in Northern Iceland seven hours before and was one of two sent to patrol some 500 miles out into the Atlantic almost due west of Land's End. Contact with the *Bismarck* had been regained after a lapse of thirty-one and a half hours.

This had been achieved by brilliant calculation on the part of the Air and Naval Staffs, whose plotting of the Bismarck's probable route was accurate enough to enable the Commander-in-Chief, Coastal Command, to design the pattern of his patrols so as to place them exactly where the enemy was most likely to be found. The sighting of the *Bismarck* at this stage was, in fact, the second principal factor that ensured her destruction, the first being the reconnaissance that had found her near Bergen and then discovered that she had sailed.

It's the Bismarck!

'George, the nickname given to the automatic pilot, was flying the aircraft at 500 feet when we saw a warship [said the pilot]. I was in the second pilot's seat when the occupant of the seat beside me, an American, said 'What the devil's that?' I stared ahead and saw a dull black shape through the mist which curled above a very rough sea. 'Looks like a battleship,' he said. I said, 'Better get closer. Go round its stern'.

I thought it might be the *Bismarck*, because I could see no destroyers round the ship and I should have seen them had she been a British warship. I left my seat, went to the wireless operator's table, grabbed a piece of paper and began to write out a signal. The second pilot had taken over from George and gone up to 1,500 feet into broken cloud.

As we came round he must have slightly misjudged his position, for instead of coming up astern we found ourselves right over the ship in an open place between the clouds. The first thing I knew about this was when two black puffs outside the starboard wing-tip appeared. In a moment we were surrounded by black puffs. Stuff began to rattle against the hull. Some of it went through and a lot more made dents in it.

I scribbled 'end of message' and handed it to the wireless operator. In between the smudges of the bursting shells I looked down on the ship, which seemed to me to be one big winking flame. She was taking violent action by turning hard to starboard, keeling well over.'

The Catalina took similar action to dodge the anti-aircraft fire. None of the crew was hit, though a piece of shell passed upwards through the floor between the two pilots as they were changing places. The only casualties occurred in the galley, where one of the crew, who was washing up the breakfast things, dropped two china R.A.F. plates and broke them.

Contact with the *Bismarck* was temporarily lost again, for the evasive action taken by the Catalina had taken her some miles from the ship. At 11.15 a.m., however, aircraft from the *Ark Royal*, now about seventy miles away, found her again, and another Coastal Command Catalina in the area was diverted from its patrol zone and reported sighting the enemy at 1.28 p.m. It kept the *Bismarck* more or less in view during the afternoon, though it lost her at intervals, owing to the bad visibility. It had to return to base at 6 p.m.

Some three hours later an event occurred which was the final factor in determining the fate of the *Bismarck*. She had been shadowed on and off throughout the day of 26 May by Coastal Command or aircraft, and now three powerful forces of the Royal Navy were closing in on her. Then, at 8.55 p.m., fifteen torpedo-carrying Swordfish from the *Ark Royal* launched an attack.

It lasted half an hour, and when it was over the *Bismarck's* steering gear was wrecked and her rudders jammed at an angle of between ten and fifteen degrees, thus causing her to turn in circles. Throughout that fierce half hour she put up a tremendous anti-aircraft barrage, firing off practically all her A.A. ammunition, but the Swordfish darted through it like flashes of lightning to score two and possibly three hits. No aircraft was lost, the only casualties being a pilot and an air gunner who were wounded.

The position of the *Bismarck* was now desperate. Despite all their efforts, her divers, who were promised the Knight Insignia of the Iron Cross if they succeeded, could only free one rudder: the other remained jammed and immovable. That night, destroyers, one of them the *Cossack*, went in close and delivered six torpedo attacks, scoring three more hits.

Dawn on 27 May found the *Bismarck* striving to make about ten knots. By now the main British force had come up, and at 8.45 a.m. the great ships opened fire. In less than an hour the *Bismarck* was a blazing wreck; but she did not surrender. The *coup de grâce* was delivered by the torpedoes of the *Dorsetshire*, and the *Bismarck* sank shortly afterwards with her colours flying.

Soon after the *Bismarck* sank, a message was received by the Commander-in-Chief, Coastal Command. 'The Admiralty,' it read, 'wish gratefully to acknowledge the part played by the reconnaissance of the forces under your command, which contributed in a large measure to the successful outcome of the recent operation.'

The Struggle for Malta

Gladiator, Fulmar, Skua, Spitfire and Hurricane

Malta was the key to the Mediterranean and the air battles of Malta reflected British fortunes from the Dunkirk days to the desert victory. From June 1940 to November 1942, the island had 3,215 air raid warnings: an average of one every seven hours for two and a half years. Axis aircraft dropped 14,000 tons of bombs, killed 1,468 civilians, destroyed or damaged 24,000 buildings, and lost 1,129 aircraft.

When Italy declared war on 10 June 1940, the island's aerial defence comprised just three Sea Gladiators, which became known as Faith, Hope and Charity. At first the Axis bombers flew in tight groups, usually despising fighter escort over a target they regarded as defenceless. But one formation of five Macchi 200 fighters also came in on the first day. Flying Officer W. J. Woods filed the first combat report on Malta:

'We sighted a formation of five S.79 enemy aircraft approaching Valetta at a height of approximately 15,000 feet. We climbed until we were slightly above them, and then Red Two delivered an attack from astern. The enemy had turned out to sea. I delivered an attack from astern and got in a good burst at a range of approximately 200 yards. My fire was returned. I then broke away and returned over the island at approximately 11,000 feet, south of Grand Harbour.

While still climbing to gain height, I observed another formation of five enemy aircraft approaching. They were at about the same height as myself. I attacked from abeam at about 150 yards and got in one good burst. The enemy started firing at me long before I opened up. This formation broke slightly but left me well behind when I tried to get in an attack from astern.

Just after that, when again climbing to gain more height, I suddenly heard machine-gun fire from behind me. I immediately went into a steep left-hand turn and saw a single-engine fighter diving and firing at me. For quite three minutes I circled as tightly as possible and got the enemy in my sight. I got in a good burst, full deflection shot and he went down in a steep dive with black smoke pouring from his tail. I could not follow him down, but he appeared to go into the sea.

Faith, Hope, and Charity

By 16 June, Faith, Hope and Charity had forced the Italians into the luxury of fighter escort. The Regia Aeronautica on that day flew in three formations, all of which the Gladiators managed to disperse. At the end of the second week of war on Malta, Berlin radio claimed that the Italian air force had 'completely destroyed the British naval base at Malta.'

Late on 22 June, after a rare raid-free day, the Italians sent an S.79 bomber to take photographs of the Grand Harbour so as to leave no doubt about this claim. Flight Lieutenant Burges reported: 'Ordered to intercept enemy aircraft reported approaching Malta. Enemy sighted at 13,000 feet when we were at 12,000 feet. Altered course to intercept and climbed to 15,000 feet and carried out stern attack from above enemy. Port engine and then starboard engine of enemy caught fire and attack was discontinued.' The Italians did not get their photographs. The bomber fell into the sea and two of the crew followed it down by parachute. These were the first Axis airmen to be brought captive to the island.

Before the end of the month, four Hurricanes landed at Malta on transit passage from Britain to Egypt. The air commodore commanding Malta obtained permission to keep them there. This was fortunate for the island, as two of the Gladiators had met with accidents on their airfield and were temporarily out of service. The Gladiators survived for many more months on active service, but the main fighter defence now passed to the Hurricane. During the darkest period of the battle Hurricanes were to be the mainstay of Malta, the single obstacle between the island and its conquest.

From then on, the service and civilian populations of Malta were determined to hold on at all costs. Convoys could still get through to Malta. And on 1 July Malta-based aircraft of the Fleet Air Arm actually struck at oil storage tanks in Sicily.

The Italians seemed surprised that they should meet any difficulty in overwhelming Malta, and decided to make an extra effort during July. A handful of fighters always met them, two or three engaging up to a score of the enemy. On 13 July, a dozen C.R.42s were engaged by a lone Hurricane and a lone Gladiator – probably the only one serviceable at the time. The Hurricane was damaged. The enemy were trying to reduce the island's fighter strength by sending over more of their own fighters. The total force of fighters operational at that particular moment amounted to one Hurricane and two Gladiators, which hung on like grim death hoping for more Hurricanes. They had literally little else but Faith and Hope.

On 16 July, after five weeks of the Battle of Malta, the R.A.F. lost its first fighter. This crashed 100 yards away from a C.R.42 brought down during the scrap. Both pilots were killed. The Italians lost a total of ten aircraft.

Enter the Luftwaffe

On 2 August 1940, H.M.S. *Argus* steamed to within 200 miles of Malta to fly off twelve Hurricanes and two Skuas. This consignment arrived safely and formed the basis for a proper fighter flight. During August the enemy turned from the dockyards to the airfields and tried to wear down the fighter reinforcements. Then came the dive-bombers, Ju 87s piloted by Italians. Twenty of these attacked the Hal Far airfield on 15 September dropping delayed action bombs. Then the arrival of the Luftwaffe on Sicilian airfields marked a more serious stage in the long battle.

On 17 November twelve more Hurricanes and two Skuas were embarked in H.M.S. *Argus*. The Italian fleet forced the carrier to put about at

the Hurricanes' extreme range from Malta. Out of twelve Hurricanes and two Skuas, only four Hurricanes and one Skua reached Luqa, Malta. The rest ran out of fuel.

Soon afterwards, the aircraft carrier H.M.S. *Illustrious* arrived in the Grand Harbour with a convoy. She was listing and badly down at the stern, having been dive-bombed by the Germans for seven hours off the island. During the next few hours, the sirens sounded for enemy reconnaissance planes several times. People and aeroplanes waited for the attack.

The plan to defend the ships was to mount a barrage over the harbour, thus confronting the enemy with a screen of fire. The dive-bombers would have to contend with this to reach their targets. Over seventy aircraft came in, between 1 p.m. and 2.45 p.m. To meet them there was only the fighter force of three Fulmars and four Hurricanes. The enemy's main target was the *Illustrious* in French Creek.

From the guns rose a box barrage of more ferocity than Malta had yet heard, amplified by the guns of the ships in the harbour. The fighters waited to catch the enemy as they came in and as they banked away from the Grand Harbour. Sometimes, the fighters followed the enemy through the blanket of barrage. An officer of the Royal Artillery saw this happen:

'I was on a light anti-aircraft gun position in the harbour area for one of these attacks, and I can still see clearly a German bomber diving through that terrific curtain of steel, followed by a Fulmar. The bomber dropped his bomb and proceeded to sneak his way out through the harbour entrance a few inches above the water. He was so low that he had to rise to clear the breakwater, which is only some 15 feet high. He was obviously wobbling badly, and as he rose the Fulmar pilot shot him down into the sea on the far side of the breakwater. The Fulmar pilot then landed at his airfield, and later I received a message from him to say that he didn't think much of our barrage. However, he never flew that particular plane again, so badly was it damaged.'

Opposite the *Illustrious*, a merchant vessel, the *Essex*, lay loaded with high-explosive torpedoes and ammunition. An enemy bomb fell straight down a funnel and burst in the engine room, the explosion being contained by the bulkheads. That was the end of one ship. Two hundred houses were wiped out by the raid and 500 damaged.

The church clock of Our Lady of Victories pointed to twenty past two for the rest of the war, a continual reminder of the air battle fought that day. On 23 January the *Illustrious* sailed east under her own power and two days later anchored in Alexandria.

February 1941 marked the start of the second assault from the air. The enemy made large-scale minelaying raids on the harbours and creeks. On 17 February the islands were raided for the eleventh night in succession, yet the harbour remained effective.

In the middle of the month, the Germans began to step up their quest for air superiority. The pilots of the small Hurricane force were losing a lot of sleep, while still having to face the sweeps of Me 109s. On 16 February two formations of Me 109s were sighted over Malta. They split up at the approach of the Hurricanes, one formation climbing above the oncoming aircraft while the other dropped below.

'While on patrol over Luqa at 20,000 feet [wrote Flight Lieutenant J. A. F. MacLachlan, who led a Hurricane flight], we were attacked by six Me 109s. As previously arranged, the flight broke away to the right and formed a defensive circle. I saw four more Me 109s coming out of the sun. Just as they came within range, I turned back towards them and they all overshot without firing. I looked very carefully but could see no more enemy aircraft above me, so I turned back to the tail of the nearest 109. I was turning well inside him and was just about to open fire when I was hit in the left arm by a cannon shell. My dashboard was completely smashed, so I bailed out and landed safely by parachute.'

MacLachlan's left arm had to be amputated. When he came out of hospital, he went out in a Magister flown by a colleague. After this he flew the plane himself and landed perfectly. A few days later, having flown a Hurricane again, he asked to rejoin his squadron. This was made possible by the fitting of an artificial arm back in Britain, after which he was to fly on many more successful operations.

Hurricane reinforcements

The raids did not decrease, but towards the end of April another twenty-three Hurricanes arrived. Having begun with only three Gladiators, the air defences at last began to look more realistic. A month later more Hurricanes flew in

– and about June the Luftwaffe left Sicily for the Russian front. There was even a Malta night fighter unit, and our Blenheim bombers attacked Syracuse.

Then the Spitfires

After the comparative calm of the latter half of 1941, the new year opened as a shocking contrast. On one of the most desperate days, 7 March, the first Spitfires appeared. The armed Spitfires flew in from the aircraft carrier *Eagle*. They numbered fifteen. They were to be used against the enemy fighter escorts in sections of four or six, while the Hurricanes dealt with the bombers.

'The Spitfires came waggling their wings as if to say 'OK boys, we're here' [wrote an R.A.F. sergeant manning a fire-tender on one of the airfields that day]. But that very same evening the gen went round that a big plot was building up over Sicily and within half an hour or so we were to see that Jerry really meant business. Standing at a vantage point in the village of Zurrieq, I saw the first waves of 88s coming all the way over the island. They dived down on Takali where the whole batch of Spits had landed. We tried to count them as they came in, but it was an utter impossibility. Straight down they went, and one could see the stuff leave the kites before it really got dark.

The guns were belting rounds up like nothing on earth; tracers filled the sky, and if things weren't so serious one could have called it a lovely sight. The din was terrific and Takali seemed to be ablaze from end to end. The lads would shout that some gun or other had stopped firing, and the crew had been knocked out. But no; they've started again pushing up rounds harder than ever. The Jerry seemed to be under orders to finish the place, and, by hell, he tried his best.'

Although the raids continued throughout the week, the Spitfires went into action and destroyed their first aircraft within three days of the raid. Detailed to intercept Me 109s, they shot down one, with two other probables. But their presence produced enemy attacks on the dispersal points, with much resultant damage to the Spitfires. By 2 April no single section of Spitfires was operational.

Meanwhile another struggle was taking place in the seas around Malta and in its harbours and docks. By April the Germans knew that they could not advance in the desert without cargoes from Europe. Malta threatened these. Air power was thus tied down in Sicily to try to neutralize Malta, which might otherwise have been diverted elsewhere.

During April 6,728 tons of bombs fell on Malta. Nearly half fell on the dockyards, and most of the rest on the three airfields of Luqa, Takali and Hal Far. In April alone 300 people were killed, and over 10,000 buildings destroyed or damaged, so the civilians suffered also. On average 170 flew over every day: waves of twelve to fifteen Ju 88s and 87s came in at intervals of a few minutes. Three raids a day became typical. During April a total of almost twelve and a half days was spent under alert.

Although one Hurricane squadron had been re-equipped with Spitfires previously, and a second in April, the Hurricane once more came to bear the brunt of the battle after many Spitfires had been lost on the ground. Sometimes a raiding party of 100 Axis aircraft would be met by only a dozen Hurricanes. Sometimes the odds were even greater.

Malta, George Cross

Malta was awarded the George Cross on 15 April. Five days later fifty-four Spitfires set out for Malta from the aircraft carrier *Wasp*, though only forty-seven actually arrived as they were virtually chased in. No sooner had they arrived than they were attacked on the ground, and many of them were 'spitchered' while they were still being refuelled, rearmed and serviced. Over 300 bombers were sent over in one day to destroy them, and by the end of the next day only eighteen were serviceable, and within three days of landing all the Spitfires had been grounded. The Germans lost nearly 200 aircraft in April, but R.A.F. losses were proportionally still worse: twenty-three Spitfires lost and fifty-seven damaged; eighteen Hurricanes lost and thirty damaged. The air raids continued unceasingly, with ever fewer fighters to counter them. Fortunately for the Maltese defences the Germans made the great mistake of easing up for a few days at the end of the month, when something else had happened to sway events – Spitfires to the rescue!

Sixty-four Spitfires were scheduled to land on the airfields from 1 a.m. onwards on Saturday 9 May. These flew off the *Wasp* and *Eagle*. But the R.A.F. had to be careful not to lose them before they could be brought to bear on the struggle.

One of the new Spitfire pilots described his day:

'Took off from the Wasp at 0645 hours. Landed at Takali at 1030 hours. The formation leader flew too fast and got his navigation all to hell, so I left them 40 miles west of Bizerta, five miles off the N. African coast, and set course for Malta, avoiding Pantellaria and Bizerta owing to fighters and flak being present there. Jettisoned the long-range tank 20 miles w of Bizerta and reached Malta with twenty gallons to spare in main tank. Of the 47 machines that flew off the Wasp one crashed into the sea on take-off, one force-landed back on to the deck as he had jettisoned his auxiliary tank in error, one landed in Algeria, one ran out of petrol between Pantellaria and Malta, one crashed on landing at Hal Far, and one crashed off Grand Harbour.

On landing at Takali I immediately removed my kit, and the machine was rearmed and refuelled. I landed during a raid and four Me 109s tried to shoot me up. Soon after landing, the airfield was bombed but without much damage being done. I was scrambled in a section of four soon after the raid, but we failed to intercept the next one, though we chased several 109s down on the deck. Ate lunch in the aircraft, as I was at the ready till dusk. After lunch we were heavily bombed again by eight Ju 88s.

Scrambled again in the same section after tea – no luck again. One Spit was shot down coming in to land and another one at the edge of the airfield. Score for the day, 7 confirmed, 7 probables and 14 damaged for the loss of 3 Spits.

The tempo of life here is just indescribable. The morale of all is magnificent – pilots, ground crews and army, but life is certainly tough. The bombing is continuous on and off all day. One lives here only to destroy the Hun and hold him at bay; everything else, living conditions, sleep, food, and all the ordinary standards of life have gone by the board. It all makes the Battle of Britain and fighter sweeps seem like child's play in comparison, but it is certainly history in the making and nowhere is there aerial warfare to compare with this.'

Spiralled downwards

The next day, the minelaying cruiser H.M.S. *Welshman* was due at Malta soon after dawn. And throughout that day the R.A.F. protected the vessel against enemy raids. Morning, afternoon and evening they came. The same pilot who described his first day on Malta had this to say about the second:

'We climbed up to 4,000 feet, and then the barrage was put up by the harbour defences and the cruiser. The c.o. dived down into it and I followed close on him. We flew three times to and fro in the barrage, trusting to luck to avoid the flak. Then I spotted a Ju 87 climbing out of the fringe of the barrage and I turned and chased him. I gave him a one-second burst of cannon and he broke off sharply to the left. At that moment another Ju 87 came up in front of my nose and I turned into him and I let him have it. His engine started to pour out black smoke and he started weaving. I kept the button pushed hard, and after a further two or three second burst with the one cannon I had left, the other having jammed, he keeled over at 1,500 feet and went into the drink.

I then spotted a 109 firing at me from behind and pulled the kite round to port, and after one and a half turns got on his tail. Before I could fire, another 109 cut across my bows from the port side and I turned straight on his tail and fired, till my cannon stopped through lack of 'ammo'. He was hit and his engine poured out black smoke, but I had to beat it as I was now defenceless and two more 109s were attacking me.

I spiralled straight down to the sea at full throttle, and then weaved violently towards land with the two 109s still firing at me. I went under the fringe of the smokescreen to try to throw them off, but when I came out the other side I found them both sitting up top waiting for me. I therefore kept right down at nought feet and steep-turned towards them, noticing the smoke from their gun ports as I did so. After about five minutes of this, I managed to throw them off. I landed back at Takali and made out my report, claiming one 87 destroyed and one Me 109 damaged.'

Turn of the tide

There were 110 Spitfire sorties and fourteen Hurricane sorties that day, 10 May 1942. They destroyed fifteen attackers, and ack-ack a further eight. Three Spitfires were lost, but two of the pilots were saved, so the *Welshman* had been protected from enemy air attack for the loss of one pilot. After that the Germans made fewer daylight raids but more by night. Their losses were still substantial.

Gradually a new plan was introduced of intercepting bombers before they could reach Malta, and this in time tilted the scales still further against the Germans. The inevitable result of this plan was that pilots and aeroplanes were liable to come down in the Mediterranean, and so the Air-Sea Rescue Service became more vital than ever. This is just one typical story from a high speed launch log:

'At 11 a.m. we had a call out in HSL 128 for a Spitfire pilot, said to have bailed out on a bearing of 160 Hal Far, about 100 yards out. Sounded like a piece of cake, for even though enemy fighters were plentiful in the vicinity, the position given was close to the island and we now had Spitfires on the job as well as Hurricanes. Getting on the given bearing, we steamed 100, 200, 300 yards – still nothing seen – and kept on going, though enemy activity was getting more and more lively overhead.

After we had steamed out about three miles, one of the escorting Hurricanes was shot down a couple of miles ahead of us. It was while we were investigating this wreckage that Jerry got closest to us, but even then the bullets only churned up the water over 100 feet away. As there was no survivor from this crash and still no sign of the original pilot for whom we had been called out, I decided to make for base, but on our way back we saw another fighter crash about six miles over to the westward and a parachute drifting down. We picked this pilot up within a few minutes of his hitting the water, and he turned out to be a Hun – a cheery soul who advised us to get back ashore before we were hurt.

As we were then fairly well out, I decided to run out and then come in on our original bearing from a distance of about ten miles, as even the worst possible estimate of distance could hardly be over ten miles out. We actually found the Spitfire pilot in his dinghy about nine miles from the land, and the German pilot insisted upon shaking hands with him as he welcomed him aboard.'

Malta was still besieged, short of food, battered and bombed. The convoys still had to claw their way to and from the island. As late as 11 October 1942, fifty-eight bombers blasted Malta, and during the next week there were nearly 250 raids by day. But on 23 October came El Alamein and sweeping success in the Western Desert. At long last, the siege was raised.

And it was from Malta that Spitfire fighter-bombers first flew, carrying 250-pounders for bombing raids on enemy airfields in Sicily. The Allies were switching from defensive to offensive in the Mediterranean as elsewhere.

The Channel Dash

Swordfish and Spitfire

Lieutenant-Commander Eugene Esmonde was serving on the aircraft carrier *Victorious* when it took part in the destruction of the *Bismarck*. At that time, the *Victorious* had not been long commissioned, and indeed some of her air crew had had hardly any battle experience when Admiral Tovey sent the *Victorious* on ahead of the British sea forces to launch an air attack with the aim of cutting the *Bismarck*'s speed. When the carrier released her nine torpedo-carrying Swordfish into a biting head wind, raging rain and low cloud on a 120-mile flight, they struggled for two hours until, late in the evening, they found the *Bismarck*. Going in under ferocious fire, they scored a direct hit with a torpedo below the bridge.

Somehow all nine of the Swordfish managed to start back towards their base ship, but their troubles were by no means over. The squadron had had scant experience of deck-landing in daylight, let alone on a black rainy Atlantic night, and the captain of the *Victorious* was understandably concerned about their safe return. It would be difficult for them even to locate the carrier, for the homing beacon aboard had failed. Signal lamps were lit instead. However, with the aid of the lamps, all nine pilots landed safely.

After the *Victorious*, Esmonde joined the *Ark Royal* in August 1941. He had been aboard the *Courageous* when she went down in 1939, and now, on 13 November 1941, another carrier was to be sunk before his eyes. Mortally hit a few miles from Gibraltar, the famous carrier limped along in two for nearly twelve hours, during which time her Swordfish squadron flew several sorties carrying members of the crew to the comparative safety of Gibraltar. A destroyer took off the rest of the 1,600 ship's company, and before the *Ark Royal* tilted too severely the last Swordfish ever to take off from the flight deck headed for Gibraltar.

Esmonde later reformed the squadron at Lee-on-Solent with seven of the officers who had been in the *Ark Royal*, and what the squadron officers lacked in experience they made up for in enthusiasm.

Early in February 1942, the Admiralty suspected that the *Scharnhorst*, *Gneisenau* and *Prinz Eugen* might break out from their French port of Brest and try to force a passage through the English Channel to their home ports in Germany. The Fleet Air Arm had a long account to settle with the *Scharnhorst* and the *Gneisenau*, for eight of the *Ark Royal*'s Skua crews had perished in an attack on the enemy battleships at Trondheim, as well as two Swordfish in an attack off the Norwegian coast in the same campaign. Although naval aircraft had sighted the two ships more than once in the Atlantic, no striking force had ever caught them. Esmonde had already asked to be allowed to lead his squadron against them if the need for such an attack ever arose.

One evening Esmonde called his squadron officers to his cabin and told them to be ready for a strike at any moment; the aircraft were prepared and armed with torpedoes. There was a 'flap' at 3 a.m. next morning and the officers were briefed, but it proved to be a false alarm – a strange coincidence in view of what was to happen.

Next morning the squadron flew to an R.A.F. station in Kent, arriving in a blizzard, and were put on five minutes' readiness. Esmonde was in fact expecting to make a night attack on the German ships, and arrangements had been made for R.A.F. fighters to accompany the Swordfish as flare-droppers. The maintenance ratings had to dig the dispersed aircraft out of the snow in the morning and run the engines three times during the day to keep them warm.

On 11 February, Esmonde went to Buckingham Palace to receive the D.S.O. he had been awarded for the *Bismarck* action. Next morning, Thursday 12 February 1942, Sub-Lieutenant (Air) B. W. Rose, R.N.V.R., was returning to the mess with his observer after a practice flight when a lorry with some of the squadron officers came tearing past. One of them shouted: 'The balloon's gone up!' It was then a few minutes after noon.

R.A.F. Headquarters had reported that the three ships had at last broken cover and appeared in the Channel, with an escort of destroyers, torpedo boats, E-boats and mine-sweepers, and a fighter escort described as 'the biggest ever seen over a naval force'.

Rose and his observer ran back to the crew room to put on their flying kit again, and just as they were ready Esmonde came rushing in to give them orders: 'Fly at 50 feet, close line astern, individual attacks, and find your own way home. We shall have fighter protection.'

The Fleet Air Arm did not waste time. Already the enemy ships would be well along the French coast and nearing the Straits of Dover. The aim was to try to intercept this massive force of more than two dozen surface craft, and attack them before they could reach the sandbanks north-east of Calais.

The six Swordfish crews climbed into their slow, torpedo-carrying biplanes, taxied out, and took off at about 12.30 p.m., grouping into two sub-flights of three each, flying in echelon. Only a few Motor Torpedo Boats, the Dover shore batteries, and ten Spitfires were able to support them, the fighters zigzagging across the course to keep their speed down to that of the Swordfish. Already by 1942, the biplanes, with their Pegasus engines and single gun turrets, were regarded as out-of-date.

By now, the German warships had passed through the Straits of Dover and were some ten miles north of Calais. According to the subsequent German account, they had left Brest with their escort of destroyers, immediately after an R.A.F. raid at 8.30 the previous night. The E-boats and mine-sweepers had joined them up-Channel, hugging the French coast. Their covering umbrella of shore-based fighters could be relieved and reinforced from the coastal airfields at short notice. As the squadron passed through the straits, the long-range batteries on the Kent coast opened fire, but the ships took evasive action. They were also able to avoid the torpedoes fired by the M.T.B.s and destroyers that tried to intercept them.

The Swordfish sighted the enemy after twenty minutes' flying time. The vessels were a mile and a half away, steaming in line ahead, with the *Prinz Eugen* leading, followed by the *Scharnhorst* and the *Gneisenau*; they were almost through the straits. Visibility had been patchy during the flight, sometimes right down, and at other times up to a couple of miles.

The force went into the attack over the destroyer screen, meeting intense anti-aircraft fire as they closed towards the capital ships. Esmonde, in aircraft No. W.5984/825 was still flying at only fifty feet when a shell ricocheted off the water and hit the belly of his Swordfish, causing him to steer an erratic course. Johnson, the air gunner of Rose's aircraft next astern, was hit.

Then the ships' guns quietened and the fighter attacks began. About fifteen Me 109s and Fw 190s dived out of the clouds onto the tails of the Swordfish, and the Spitfire escort became involved in a general dogfight. An Fw 190 ripped off the top of the main plane of Esmonde's aircraft and he went straight down into the sea.

Rose was attacked both from ahead and astern, at a range of some 200 yards. He dodged as well as he could while his observer, Sub-Lieutenant (Air) E. Lee, R.N.V.R., stood up in the after cockpit and shouted 'Port' or 'Starboard' as the attacks came in. They could see the tracer bullets streaming past, and the Swordfish was being hit continually. Moreover, the constant evasive action slowed down its advance, and to make matters worse there was no one to work the rear gun. Johnson had been either knocked unconscious or killed instantaneously, and Lee could not move his body.

In spite of Lee's watchfulness Rose was hit by splinters from a cannon shell that struck the bulkhead behind his seat. Now leading, and with his engine faltering, he decided they must attack without delay. He selected the leading ship and, getting as good a position as he could, dropped his torpedo at a range of about 1,200 yards and saw it running well. It was difficult to observe results, but directly he had made his attack the fighters ceased to pay any further attention to him, concentrating instead on the others. One Swordfish had two Focke-Wulfs on its tail, their flap and undercarriages down to retard their speed, attacking whichever way the pilot turned.

Swordfish afire

The third aircraft, piloted by Sub-Lieutenant (Air) C. M. Kingsmill, R.N.V.R., had the two top cylinders of its engine shot away. The engine and the upper port wing caught fire, yet the air gunner, Leading Airman D. A. Bunce, continued to engage the enemy fighters and saw one crash into the sea. Although all the crew of this Swordfish were wounded, Kingsmill kept control long enough to aim his torpedo in the direction of the second enemy ship, then turned with difficulty and tried to land near some vessels, which turned out to be E-boats. They opened fire on him, but he kept flying until his engine finally cut out. The Swordfish crashed on the water a few hundred yards from some British M.T.B.s and eventual rescue, though the crew had first to take to the icy water because their dinghy had been destroyed by fire.

The three Swordfish in the second sub-flight were piloted by Lieutenant (Air) J. C. Thompson, R.N., Sub-Lieutenant (Air) C. R. Wood, R.N., and Sub-Lieutenant (Air) P. Bligh, R.N.V.R. They were seen crossing the destroyer screen to attack, taking violent evasive action, but proceeding steadily towards the enemy capital ships. Nothing further was seen of them after that.

As soon as Rose had dropped his torpedo he tried to make as much height as possible and went out on the port wing of the destroyer screen. He had climbed to 1,200 feet when Lee told him petrol was pouring out of the starboard side. It was obvious that he could not reach the English coast and he decided to make for some M.T.B.s. He was within four miles of them when his engine cut out, but, undeterred, he glided down towards the sea, pulled his stick well back and pancaked. As he said later, 'The Swordfish sat down very nicely.'

Rose climbed out of his cockpit into the sea, while Lee tried, unsuccessfully, to remove Johnson, the air gunner, from the after cockpit. Rose could not help him because his left arm was useless, though when the dinghy was washed out into the sea Rose recovered it and got it upright. Lee held it while Rose climbed into it, then went back to the aircraft to make another attempt to remove Johnson. He could not do so, and had to leave him. There was no doubt that he was dead.

Lee then joined Rose in the dinghy, but the sea was choppy and it soon filled with water, which they tried to bail out, without much success, with their flying helmets. Then, from their emergency gear, they took out the marine distress signals and the aluminium dust-markers. (The dust formed a silver pool around the dinghy and could be seen at a distance.) But they flung the dust to windward and it blew back on them, so that they looked like a couple of shining tin soldiers. However, they could use the empty tins for bailing out the dinghy, and when it was dry they fired the distress signals. Two M.T.B.s then closed in on the dinghy. By that time they had been in the water for an hour and a half. Rose was suffering severely from his wounds, and both he and Lee were numb with cold.

There were only five survivors from the Swordfish striking force; Lee was the only one unwounded. Having made his report to the naval authorities, he apologized for having to hurry away, but, as he explained, he was now acting senior officer of the little squadron.

The four surviving officers were awarded the D.S.O., and the air gunner, Leading Airman Bunce, the C.G.M. The crews who lost their lives received mentions in despatches, while Eugene Esmonde was awarded the V.C. posthumously.

Bomber Offensive
Wellington, Stirling and Halifax

Soon after Fighter Command had won the Battle of Britain and beaten the Blitz, Bomber Command was on the offensive against Germany. These two examples are typical of the conditions encountered and overcome. One is the story of a single bomber in close-up; the other, an account of a 1,000-aircraft raid.

First the flight of Wellington T for Tommy. At 11.30 p.m. one summer night in the middle years of the war, aircraft T.2619 took off in thick darkness on an operational flight to Germany. Known to all concerned as T for Tommy, the Wellington had seven 500-pound bombs on board and its crew were all sergeants. Saich, who came from Dunmow, was the pilot; Telling, an Epsom man, the second pilot; the navigator was Smitten, a Canadian from Edmonton; while the remaining three members were an Englishman, Trott, from Sheffield, and two more Canadians – Hooper from Vancouver, the front gunner, and English from Picton, Nova Scotia, the rear gunner. Their target lay in the German port of Bremen.

At first it seemed they would have trouble finding the target at all. Just before T for Tommy reached the city, however, it came out of the clouds into a clear sky intersected by the sharp beams of searchlights. A slight haze hung over the roof-tops 11,000 feet below, but Sergeant Smitten found the target and Sergeant Saich began his bombing run. The time was 1.40 a.m. One bomb was released. Then the wheeling, probing lights caught and held T for Tommy in a cone which grew in size and intensity as more and more beams concentrated upon the aircraft.

As soon as the enemy ground defences got it in their sights and range, the bomber became the target of intense and accurate fire. Two shells burst at zero range, one just behind and below the rear turret, the other inside the fuselage itself, level with the leading edge of the tailplane.

The first shell wounded Sergeant English, the rear gunner, in the shoulder and hand, and cut the hydraulic controls to the turret so that it could no longer be turned, except by the slow process of cranking it. Fragments of the other shell riddled the rear part of the fuselage, and set on fire the fabric covering it and the tail fin, which is the special characteristic of the Wellington.

In a few seconds, T for Tommy looked like a flying torch, thus presenting the kind of target that anti-aircraft gunners pray for – and aircraft crew pray against. The enemy jumped at it. The flames seemed to be the signal for every ground gun in the target zone to fire directly at them. And all this time, the rear gunner was in the blazing end of the torch.

Sergeant Saich, the pilot, took violent evasive action and actually managed to throw the German gunners off their aim – at least momentarily. While he was doing so, Smitten, the navigator, went to the help of English in the rear turret. He made his way down the rocking, shell-split fuselage till he was stopped short by the fire separating him from the turret. For the moment he could go no further.

He crawled back a little way, snatched a fire-extinguisher, and returned to the fire in the fuselage, which he subdued. Above him the fin still flamed. He sprayed it with all that was left of the methyl-bromide in the extinguisher, thrusting it through the hot framework of the fuselage from which the fabric had been burned. Eventually Smitten somehow reached the turret.

By the time he got there, Sergeant English was making preparations to abandon the aircraft by swinging the turret round into the beam position. A rear gunner bailed out by turning his turret until the steel doors through which he entered and left it faced the open air to port or starboard – instead of the interior of the fuselage. He then opened the doors and threw himself out backwards.

English was about to do this when Smitten reached him. He had opened the doors, and now they refused to close. Smitten went back and returned with a light axe. He leaned out through a hole beneath the fin, which he had just saved from burning, and, with the wind of the slipstream tearing at him, hacked away at the doors till they fell off. At that stage English was able to rotate his turret by the hand gear. As soon as the gaping hole where the doors had hung coincided with the end of the fuselage, he extricated himself and entered the aircraft – or what was left of it.

While all this was going on astern, more trouble broke out forward. The Wellington was hit again, and a shell splinter set light to the flares carried in the port wing. These were for use in an emergency, when a forced landing might have to be made in darkness – the sort of emergency that actually existed at that precise moment. The flares burned so brightly that Saich thought the port

engine was on fire. He promptly turned off its petrol, opened the throttle fully and switched off. Soon the flames died down, for the flares had burned their way through the fabric of the mainplane and fallen from the aircraft.

Realizing what had happened Saich turned on the petrol again and restarted the engine. At his orders, Telling, the second pilot, crouched beside the main spar behind the wireless cabin, pumping all the oil that could be extracted from a riddled auxiliary tank. T for Tommy was still under the most massed ack-ack fire, and one of the shell splinters wounded Telling. Their hail continued to tear through the fuselage.

Already by this time many people would have thought it only sensible to abandon the aircraft, but yet a further misfortune was to befall the Wellington. At the moment when the Germans scored their first hit, the bomb doors were actually open, for the aircraft had been completing its first bombing run-up and one of the bombs had just gone down on Bremen.

That anti-aircraft shell caused such havoc that it became impossible either to close the bomb doors or to release the remaining six bombs, since the hydraulic pipes had been punctured and the electrical wiring to the slips severed. And each of the bombs weighed 500 pounds. As well as all this, and the damage to the fuselage, rear turret, rudder and fin, there was a large hole knocked by a shell in the starboard tank.

Hole in the wing

In this extraordinary condition, T for Tommy began to head for base. The chances of making it seemed slim. With the bomb doors open and a heavy load still on board, the aircraft was very hard to control. Saich's task was not made any easier by the hole in the wing. The draught hissed through this hole, blanketing the starboard aileron, which was virtually useless. Nevertheless, Saich held sternly to the homeward course given him by Smitten. T for Tommy choked its way back over the North Sea.

Its speed had been cut to an alarmingly low level, and the petrol gauges registered empty for some two hours out of the four on that memorable return route. They flew on and on, over nearly 300 miles of sea, until at 5.35 a.m. the Wellington crossed the East Anglian coast dead on track. With dry land beneath him once more, Sergeant Saich determined to make a forced landing, for he thought that at any moment the engines would splutter to stop for lack of fuel.

The sky was beginning to pale as Saich picked out a barley field where it seemed to him a successful landing might be made. In the half-light he did not see the obstruction poles set up in the field to hinder an enemy airborne invasion.

Saich now set about making his perilous descent. The flaps would not work, and when he came to pump the undercarriage down with the emergency hydraulic hand-pump, he found that owing to loss of oil it would only push the tail wheel and one of the main wheels into their positions. T for Tommy came in to land, a little lopsided to take full advantage of the one sound wheel. On touching down, the aircraft swung round, but an obstruction pole violently arrested its motion. It shuddered and then came abruptly to rest on its belly with its back broken. Save for many bumps and bruises, none of the crew suffered further.

But T for Tommy was little more than a wreck. It had flown back to that East Anglian barley field with a huge hole in its starboard wing, with uncounted smaller holes in its fuselage, with nine feet of fabric burned entirely away forward from the rear turret, with half the fin and half the rudder in the same condition. Yet it flew home.

The story of T for Tommy is not unique, nor even unusual. If it were, the bomber build-up could not have continued as it did. Many other aircraft of Bomber Command sustained similar damage and survived at least long enough to bring their crews back to Britain. Not only Wellingtons, but Blenheims, Hampdens, Whitleys, Stirlings, Halifaxes, Manchesters and Lancasters.

1000-bomber blitz

So from the story of one bomber to a story of many: a 1,000-bomber blitz on Cologne. Such massive attacks required much planning and preparation. Bomber Command were employing a new technique of concentrating a large force of aircraft for a short time over a single target. The effect of this was to dislocate, if not paralyse, all ground defences and air raid precautions. Before these raids, however, there was often a steady softening up process.

The first example of these new stupendous-scale tactics was the attack on the Renault works in France. At this period, the Ruhr suffered eight heavy raids involving 1,555 aircraft altogether, besides three small attacks. In the same spell, Cologne was visited four times by a total of 559 aircraft. The damage done to the city was considerable. In the Nippes district, an industrial

part, about 75,000 square yards occupied by workshops were damaged. Heavy bombs completely destroyed buildings nearby, covering an area of 6,000 square yards. The Franz Clouth rubber works, covering 168,000 square yards, were rendered useless, much of it being levelled to the ground. To the east of the Rhine, the bombers hit a chemical factory and buildings alongside. Severe damage was also done to the centre of Cologne. All this was confirmed by evidence in camera.

Then came the night of 30–31 May 1942. One thousand bombers brought chaos to Cologne. At the hour of take-off the whole staff of one particular station was assembled around the aerodrome. The station commander himself sent off the aircraft. Two flare-paths were laid and the Wellingtons were despatched simultaneously from both paths with only 300 yards between them. The first eleven got away in eight minutes: one every forty-four seconds. Some miles to the north, forty-three Halifaxes became airborne a little later. A few miles to the east air crews climbed into their Stirlings. Scenes such as these were taking place throughout eastern England. The Wellingtons arrived first over Cologne, followed closely by the Stirlings.

'When we got there [said the wing commander of a squadron of Wellingtons], we saw many fires which had not yet taken real hold, but I thought it had all the makings of a successful raid. It was easy enough to see the city, for we could pick out the Rhine and the bridges quite clearly. There was little or no opposition over the target, I think because there were so many aircraft that the ground defences could not cope with them. We did meet with opposition on the outskirts but it was very indiscriminate. Before I left I saw fires growing larger and larger.'

It was then that the Stirlings arrived. Flying with them was Air Vice-Marshal Baldwin, commanding the group to which they belonged.

'The weather forecast [he said], made it uncertain almost up to the last moment whether we should start. We had not been flying very long before we met much low cloud, and this depressed me. The front gunner got a pin-point on an island off the Dutch coast but the weather was still somewhat thick and there was an Alpine range of cloud to starboard. Suddenly, 30 or 40 miles from Cologne, I saw the ground and then the flak. It grew clearer and clearer until near the city visibility was perfect. First I saw a lake, gleaming in the moonlight, then I could see fires beginning to glow, and then searchlights which wavered and flak coming up in a haphazard manner.

The sky was full of aircraft all heading for Cologne. I made out Wellingtons, Hampdens, a Whitley and other Stirlings. We sheared off the city for a moment, while the captain decided what would be the best way into the target. It was then that I caught sight of the twin towers of Cologne Cathedral, silhouetted against the light of three huge fires that looked as though they were streaming from open blast furnaces.

We went in to bomb, having for company a Wellington to starboard and another Stirling to port. Coming out we circled the flak barrage and it was eight minutes after bombing that we set course for home. Looking back, the fires seemed like rising suns and this effect became more pronounced as we drew further away. Then, with the searchlights rising from the fires, it seemed that we were leaving behind us a huge representation of the Japanese banner. Within nine minutes of the coast we circled to take a last look. The fires then resembled distant volcanoes.'

Cauldron of Cologne

When the Halifaxes arrived, the raid had already been going on for an hour. Latecomers could see the cauldron of Cologne sixty miles distant, first as a dull red glow over a large area of ground. The captain of one Halifax and his navigator both thought that the fire they were flying towards was too enormous to be anything but a specially elaborate diversion created by the Germans. The pilot of another Halifax thought that a heath or a whole forest must be ablaze.

But ten miles off they saw that the great glow came from a town on fire, and as they flew nearer still they could see more and more loads of incendiaries burning in long, narrow rectangles composed of pinpoints of bright white patches, each of which swiftly blossomed into a rose of fire. Like the others, the Halifaxes identified the target easily by the bridges over the Rhine.

One captain reported: 'So vast was the burning that ordinary fires on the outskirts of the city or outside it, which I should usually describe as very big, looked quite unimportant. It was strange to see the flames reflected on our aircraft. It looked at times as though we were on fire ourselves, with the red glow dancing up and down on the wings.'

For several days reconnaissance aircraft could not photograph Cologne. The smoke of the burning ruins was still too thick. It was not until 5 June that good pictures were taken. When intelligence examined these prints, the damage revealed was realized to be very great..

Cathedral unscathed

Cologne was a city of 750,000 people, the third largest in Germany. The total area of complete destruction caused on 30–31 May amounted to 2,904,000 square yards, compared to exactly ten per cent of that area damaged or destroyed in the four former raids. Of the area laid waste, about half was in the centre of the city. The cathedral appeared to be unscathed, except for damage to windows, but 250 factory buildings and workshops were either wiped out or badly damaged.

A significant feature of the photographs taken on 5 June was that they disclosed what appeared to be a dead city. An air raid warning would have cleared the streets while the pictures were actually being taken, but there were no signs of trains, trams, buses or cars. Apart from the material damage, the casualties caused to the population were bound to be heavy too.

The attack on Cologne was followed two nights later by a raid on the Ruhr in much the same strength. Here, too, Bomber Command caused catastrophic damage and fires. In these large raids our losses averaged under four per cent of the aircraft used. Although that sounds moderate enough, four per cent of 1,000 bombers was forty aircraft, plus the precious lives of possibly several hundred air crew.

In the attack on the Ruhr, a Halifax was caught by searchlights over Essen and heavily shelled. The port outer engine went out of action and the aircraft was held for fifteen minutes in a cone of some fifty beams. A shell splinter broke the window in front of the captain and blinded him in one eye. On the way home, an Me 110 night-fighter jumped on the crippled bomber, but the rear gunner drove off the intruder, setting its starboard engine aflame. Near Dunkirk, searchlights once more picked up the Halifax and flak knocked out the inner starboard engine. The bomber got back on two engines.

On the next night, the Ruhr received another attack. Then it was Bremen's turn, then a night's pause, then the Ruhr again, then Emden, then Bremen. So it went on night after night.

Duel in the Stratosphere

Spitfire

Above 35,000 feet, without a pressure cabin, a man must struggle to remain conscious even with the help of oxygen. He can suffer not only from the intense cold but also from temporary paralysis of the limbs, expanding gases which distend the intestines, and sometimes from 'the bends' – an affliction which deep sea divers can also experience, where all the joints of the body are gripped by a pain said to be more intense than any other. Great height also has a temporary effect on a man's mind, plunging him into despondency against his will.

One day in the summer of 1942 Flying Officer G. W. H. Reynolds, D.F.C., was flying a Spitfire which had been modified and stripped of most things save its guns. He sighted a Ju 86 reconnaissance aircraft with two men sitting securely in a pressure cabin in the nose. He was just north of Cairo and he pursued it towards Alexandria then out to sea at an ever-increasing height. At 37,000 feet he almost reached it and began to zigzag back and forth just below in order not to overshoot. The Ju 86 zigzagged in the same way, trying to stay just above the Spitfire and force it to lose a little height on each turn.

The long slow duel in the rarefied atmosphere proceeded in this manner until Reynolds was at a height of 40,000 feet. He realized then that he could not get any higher until he had used some more petrol to lighten the aircraft. He started to calculate how much petrol he could use and how far out to sea he could go before he would be forced to turn back in order to reach home safely. He had abandoned his Mae West life-saving jacket and his dinghy to save weight, keeping only a parachute.

In the middle of these calculations he temporarily blacked out, having just sufficient time to turn his oxygen tap to full emergency to bring himself round again. He then slowly forced the Spitfire higher still. At 42,000 feet he was practically level with the Ju 86, slowly closing. At a range of fifty yards he opened fire. Flame and grey smoke whipped backwards from the starboard engine of the enemy aircraft, which banked sharply to the left. Reynolds had intended to follow, but his Spitfire began not to function properly and he fell nearly 10,000 feet very quickly. The pilot's own physical endurance was in any case practically exhausted. He described his condition thus: 'I had been experiencing great pain at that height, as I was over 40,000 feet for nearly half an hour and felt rather ill. Added to this, my petrol and oxygen were low and I wished to get home as quickly as possible. I landed at base with five gallons of petrol left.'

He did not know when he landed whether or not he had destroyed the Ju 86 but its loss was afterwards confirmed. The first stratosphere reconnaissance aircraft had been shot down.

Above 40,000 feet

The destruction of this Ju 86 was the first success in a struggle between the German stratosphere reconnaissance aircraft of Egypt – such reconnaissance was the only daylight activity over that country that the Luftwaffe usually dared attempt – and a small group of test pilots and engineers of the R.A.F., who maintained that these high-flying Germans, inaccessible to any other weapon, could be reached and destroyed by a modified Spitfire.

The pilots who undertook this task were not young men. Reynolds, the man who destroyed the first Ju 86, was approaching forty years of age, yet he flew above 40,000 feet some twenty-five times within a month. His first success came only after much trial and endurance, but the three other Ju 86 aircraft which the Germans possessed for this reconnaissance work were soon to be destroyed as the first had been.

The enemy flew, however, at ever-increasing heights. The last one was pursued to nearly 50,000 feet. This one fell also to Reynolds. He had been higher than 45,000 feet for more than an hour: his whole cockpit, instrument panel, control column and perspex were thickly coated with ice; his body was racked with pain and his arms temporarily paralysed, and his eyesight also failing with weakness. When he met the Ju 86 at a distance of only 100 yards but at a height of 50,000 feet, he was physically incapable of firing his guns; yet the enemy turned and fled towards the sea. Reynolds manoeuvred his Spitfire to follow it by moving the position of his body in the delicately balanced aircraft. He caught the enemy plane once more, far out over the Mediterranean, and managed to move his hands sufficiently to press the firing button. The Ju 86 was destroyed. The Spitfire completed much of the journey back to base in a powerless glide.

When the pilot started to glide home on that flight he glanced round and below at a remarkable panorama. He could see the whole of the eastern Mediterranean spread out like a map beneath him. To the west he could see past Benghazi into the Gulf of Sirte; to the east the coastline of Palestine and Syria with the mountains beyond. Behind him lay unrolled the island-sprinkled Aegean. In front lay Egypt revealed at one glance from the coast to beyond Cairo, and the length of the Suez Canal from Port Said to Suez. Down there in the desert the army was fighting it out. The decisive twelve months were from February 1942 to January 1943. By the summer of 1942 the new air weapon had been tested and proved. During the retreat to El Alamein, R.A.F. Middle East held off the Luftwaffe, shielded the army, and battled grimly to protect the seaborne convoys.

The Air Battle of El Alamein

Bisley, Beaufighter, Hurricane, Kittyhawk, Spitfire and Wellington

The second Battle of El Alamein was the turning point of the desert war in North Africa. Rommel's German and Italian army was routed. It was Britain's first great land victory of the war. In the run-up to the battle, and during it, air forces played a significant role.

At 10 p.m. on 23 October the first wave of more than seventy bombers and flare-dropping aircraft switched the nightly attack away from the enemy landing grounds onto his troop positions all along the battle front. More than thirty Hurricanes trained in night flying started at Alamein and strafed as far back as Fuka.

The bombers kept on throughout the night, and the usual fires and explosions broke out in the desert below. There was one fire in the south which threw smoke to 3,000 feet, while in the north a large ammunition dump was blown. At first the aircraft were met with strong anti-aircraft fire, but later in the night it dwindled. The enemy gunners' attention was distracted elsewhere. Suddenly the battle line sparkled with gun flashes. For twenty minutes 800 Allied guns fired continuously along the front. The artillery had opened fire, and the

sappers and infantry were moving steadily forwards into the enemy minefields, storming Miteiriya Ridge. By dawn they had made and held gaps in the minefields.

They had been assisted by a few light bombers which flew at a low level across the minefields and laid smokescreens at the points of assault. Others laid them at points where no assault was intended, so as to confuse the enemy. One laid a smokescreen along a beach off which some British warships were manoeuvring with a great show of gunfire and commotion. So well did they deceive the enemy that next day Rome radio reported repulsing with heavy losses a British landing which had not been attempted!

Nearly 1,000 sorties

It had become a tradition of the Desert Air Force that on critical days of land warfare it should create a new record in the air. It did so on 24 October, the first full day of the land assault. The total number of sorties flown during the day was nearly 1,000. The whole weight was flying against the battle area, chiefly just west of the two gaps in the minefields. There were two smaller raids on Daba landing grounds. After the days and nights of attack sustained by the Luftwaffe, they thought more of warding the bombs from their air dispersal areas than of intervening in this first day of full battle. Some Messerschmitts and Macchis made a few half-hearted attacks, but these amounted to nothing compared with the display of Allied air power. In fact there were plenty of targets for the Luftwaffe since all our armour lay behind the minefields, waiting for the gaps to be enlarged sufficiently for it to pass through, but the Stukas did not come.

The chief opposition to the Allied bombers came from the German ground gunners. Having no tanks to meet at that time, they swung their guns upwards and filled the sky with shells. Six bombers and five fighters were shot down. It was the heaviest bomber loss the British had ever suffered in fighter-escorted raids. On the other hand, it was the heaviest bombing assault the light squadrons had ever delivered.

All day long, dust clouds hung over the landing grounds, created by the wheels at take-off. Ground crews toiled on, air crews took scant rest. They had the moral fillip of knowing that this was the first ground assault assisted by an air offensive on this scale. As they flew, the air crews gazed down at countless flashes of gunfire. Little white puffs of exploding shells spattered the desert air below them like 'handfuls of flung rice'. By midday pilots were already reporting areas of broken trucks, many ablaze, some burned out and still smouldering.

That night the Wellington crews could see battles being fought beneath them in the moonlight. Somewhere down there the infantry had widened the gaps and the tanks and guns were passing through. Bombs started many fires ahead of them, one by the coast burning fiercely for five hours. It was dawn before the last Wellington drew away. By then, the tanks and guns were all west of the first line of the enemy minefields and the infantry solidly held the bridge in the rear.

By daylight on 25 October, the British Eighth Army held a bulge in the north of the Alamein line a mile or two away from the coast. This bulge was nicknamed 'the fist'. Away to the south the attack had been sufficient to pin down the enemy airmen opposing it, but the commanding Himeimat Ridge had not been taken. From 'the fist' down to Qattara, the line ran more or less straight, due north to south.

On that day, the second of the land battle, the Luftwaffe did manage to make some sort of a challenge, but it cost them seven Messerschmitts destroyed and many more probables, while the British lost one Kittyhawk. The challenge was sufficent to switch a lot of the light bombing strength back on Daba and Fuka, but insufficient to cut down the overall programme by a single sortie. Nor was it enough to curb the Beaufighters which were ranging the back areas, shooting up supplies.

Seven Beaufighters found a merchant ship and a destroyer which had nearly succeeded in reaching Tobruk. They lay only a mile offshore and a few miles west of the port. The cannon attack of the Beaufighters left both vessels with smoke drifting upwards, but did not sink them. Having shot down two Ju 88s and a Dornier flying boat the Beaufighters hurried back to their base to lead out a striking force of bombers and torpedo-carriers. The torpedoes missed, but a bomb from a Bisley blew the merchant ship to pieces and she sank in a few minutes. One of the Beaufighters shot down two Italian C.R.42s, obsolete fighters whose very presence indicated the straits of the enemy air forces.

Shortly afterwards another force of eight Beaufighters cut into the enemy air supply route from Crete to the battle. They found some thirty-five Ju 52 transports escorted by six twin-engine Me 110s a few miles north of Tobruk.

Some of the R.A.F. fighters held off the Me 110s, shooting one of them down, while the rest went for the Junkers. They destroyed at least four of them.

The battle on the ground was taking a definite shape by 26 October. 'The fist' had wedged its way more firmly into the enemy's face, broadening out to the north and south. British troops held the whole of Miteiriya Ridge, and the tanks were embattled in strong defensive positions against which the enemy was permitted to wear out his armour. In the northern sector alone, some seventy enemy tanks had already been lost, one armoured division being reduced after only twenty-four hours' fighting to about five runners.

Another German division had been brought up from the south by a night march and was put into battle together with the 90th Light, veterans of Rommel's Afrika Korps. As they moved at night they were bombed by the R.A.F.; as they tried to form up by day they were bombed again. There were nine full-scale bombing raids during the day, during which not one bomber was lost, while numerous formations of fighter-bombers slipped down to the south, wiping out four tanks and two armoured cars.

High over the battle swept the Spitfires, still firmly holding their front line over Daba. The Kittyhawks darted far past that line, and fired several petrol convoys on the coast road around Sidi Barrani. The Luftwaffe was still trying and still losing. During the day seventeen enemy aircraft were shot down by British fighters.

Afrika Korps target

But the greatness of that day, 26 October, lay out to sea off the Tobruk coast, where British air power destroyed a whole convoy. Next day ashore the enemy army were gathered together to attempt five counter-attacks. The twenty-eighth October was probably the decisive day, even though the battle was fought furiously for several days after that. Within the space of two and a half hours the R.A.F. carried out seven full-scale bombing raids on the Afrika Korps, dropping eighty tons of bombs in an area measuring some three miles by two. Pattern after pattern of bomb bursts spread from all directions across this area of concentration. Six times the German tank crews broke hastily and scattered across the desert; six times they reformed. The seventh time they did not reform. There was no counter-attack by the Afrika Korps on the Eighth Army. The enemy did not try to take the initiative again in the Battle of El Alamein.

About a week later the enemy retreat was in full flood. One bomber pilot said: 'As we swept the road, we saw it packed with transport. But every vehicle was stopped, and everywhere there were tiny trails of dust where crews were running into the desert. Every bomber in our formation turned and sailed down the road, spilling bombs on vehicles and men. I never saw such a scene of destruction.'

South of the Alamein position in a few days R.A.F. bombers would be searching for Italians, not to bomb them but to drop them water and food so that they would not die before they could be taken prisoner.

Meanwhile the main preoccupation was the road. By dusk whole lengths of it were blazing with fires enough for the Wellingtons to attack all night. This was the night they had been waiting for: they called it 'Bombers' Benefit'. The enemy vehicles were all concentrated around the thin ribbon of the coast road, lit by the fires that were destroying them. The Wellingtons started about sixty fresh fires along the stretch of road that runs through Daba. The truck columns continued to drive westwards throughout the night traversing the area of fiercest attack under cover of darkness.

The road was so crowded that it reminded one pilot of the Brighton road on August Bank Holiday in days of peace, or the Epsom road on Derby Day. The bombers came down low to bomb, then lower still to open fire with machine guns.

'As we came in to drop our first stick the vehicles careered madly off the road. It looked absolutely crazy. I saw one overturn as it went over the bank. We could see troops leaping out and running away like cockroaches. They were colliding and jumping head first into patches of scrub or any hole they could find.'

'Our first stick cracked right across the lorries at right angles. We could see some of the lorries coming up in the air . . . We went in low over a tented encampment and could see our tracer cutting through the canvas.'

It was 4 November. After twelve days and nights the retreat had become a rout.

The Dam-Busters
Lancaster

On 17 March 1943, No. 5 Bomber Group headquarters received a letter from Bomber Command telling them of a new mine weapon intended to be used against 'a large dam in Germany'. The attack had to be made during May, and a new squadron was formed to carry it out.

Four days later, this squadron started to form at Scampton, while the twenty Lancasters it would receive were being built. The whole project was both top secret and top priority. Everyone picked for it had to be top grade, too, air and ground crews alike. The personnel had to be chosen first of all, before the modified Lancasters were ready. The man chosen to command the new squadron was Guy Gibson. All he himself knew about the project at that stage was that it would involve low-level flying across country, and training started along these lines at once on standard Lancasters. All twenty crews reached Scampton before the end of the month, within ten days of the squadron starting to form.

All they had yet learned was that they would have to fly at 100 feet and at 240 miles an hour. A mine would have to be dropped from each bomber within forty yards of the precise point of release. They went into training over reservoir lakes in Wales and the Midlands, for only six weeks were left to perfect this demanding technique. This ability to fly at 100 to 150 feet over water in the dark, and to navigate and drop mines accurately as well, was the first key factor in the operation. There were many more, not the least of them being able to avoid enemy fighters and ack-ack in the target area.

But Gibson did not yet know this target area, so he was literally flying in the dark. Then he met the inventor of the mines, Mr B. N. Wallis – later famous as Barnes Wallis – who told him roughly how the mines would work. They would bounce along the water towards their target. The whole project became daily more fantastic.

Meanwhile Gibson and his crew practised flying over Derwentwater reservoir, in Yorkshire, which bore resemblances to the conditions expected over the ultimate targets. After some trial runs by day Gibson discovered that he could estimate his altitude and direct a bomb at the specified speed of aircraft with reasonable accuracy. But by night he only barely escaped actually striking the gloomy invisible water of the reservoir. And the attack was to be carried out at night. They would have to learn a lot in the coming weeks. One of the many problems involved was solved when an accurate range-finder was devised which enabled the squadron to keep within a rough twenty-five yards of their target, and so within the forty yards' tolerance allowed.

The following day Gibson was let into the secret. They were to attack the great Ruhr dams of Germany: Mohne, Sorpe and Eder. The main target was the Mohne Dam, 830 yards long, 150 feet high and 140 feet thick at its base – of sheer concrete and masonry. If Gibson and his squadron could smash one or more of these dams the havoc caused to the enemy industries and communications would be tremendous.

Mines that bounce

Apart from the difficulty of flying to the rigid requirements vital for the success of the plan, there was one other problem: the mine had not yet had its full-scale trials! The first such trial came in mid-April when an inert mine was dropped from one of the modified Lancasters at the required height of 150 feet over water. The outer casing of the mine disintegrated as soon as it struck the sea off the Dorset coast. No time was lost in strengthening the casing, but this made no difference to the trials and the mine still shattered.

Gibson too had his worries, just as fundamental as the setbacks for Barnes Wallis. They found it impossible to fly at exactly 150 feet over the water and maintain that height accurately. Then a backroom boy found an answer: to train two spotlights downwards from the nose and belly of the bomber so that their beams would meet at 150 feet below the Lancaster, making a spot where they intersected. In this way, with the help of a couple of Aldis lamps, the aircraft could be flown within a few feet of any required height simply by keeping the spotlight at water level.

The next panic came when the inventor found that they could only expect effectiveness from the modified mine if it were dropped from sixty feet, not 150. Without the spotlight device, this would have been quite out of the question. By the time they had put in some practice at sixty feet May had arrived.

Early in May, an inert mine was dropped from the new height of sixty feet and operated successfully; then an active mine, which went off exactly as expected. While this aspect went well, just one more problem presented itself at the operational end. A complicated signalling system had to be worked out to control about twenty bombers over several tricky targets. The answer was very high frequency radio-teleplone sets, twenty in number. These arrived on 7 May, but a lot of routine testing and procedure had to be accomplished before the actual attack. This had been done by 9 May, except for minor adjustments.

The nearness of the operation had suddenly been brought home to them all by the dress rehearsals, the first of which was timed for the night of 6 May – and a film company was actually called on to assist by building dummy structures in the Uppingham and Colchester reservoirs, so that the squadron had something tangible for a target as they roared in during their dress rehearsal raid.

Even this stage had not been reached without further hazards and headaches, for a few days earlier half of the dozen Lancasters in one trial had sustained bad damage, with rear turrets dented, elevations broken, and fins bent. The trouble occurred because the aircraft had been flying a few feet too low, and though the mines they dropped were only inert, they had caused gigantic splashes as they struck the water, which had affected the bombers flying at 232 miles an hour.

On 15 May, Gibson got word at last: 'Be prepared to take off tomorrow.' He sat up late that evening committing the detailed operation to paper – just in case none of them got back. They had been so busy training that the danger of the mission might have partially escaped some of them, especially since it was only on the following morning that the air crews knew the complete plan.

Skimmed over the sea

On 16 May, at 9.28 p.m., the first of nineteen Lancasters took off. The main force of nine would go for the Mohne Dam and then, if it was destroyed before all their mines had gone, they would fly to the Eder. The second force of five was to head for the Sorpe Dam, while a third force of five was to form a reserve to fill in any gap, according to how the operation progressed.

They skimmed over the sea towards the Continent at a mere sixty feet or so, and went still lower after they crossed the Dutch coast.

Moonlight helped them, but navigation at that altitude proved hard.

Gibson gave his own account of the whole operation in his book *Enemy Coast Ahead*, including the difficulty of flying so low by night. He and the other two Lancasters in his immediate section of three hurtled overland, rolling right and left to confuse the defences. No guns opened fire. But in a couple of minutes they found themselves over the sea again! They had flown over one of the several islands they had tried to avoid, and instead of being inland were only now crossing the real Dutch coast. By good chance none of the ack-ack guns on the island had opened fire on them. On their fresh course, Gibson's bomb-aimer had to shout to them regularly over the intercom to lift the aircraft to avoid trees or high tension cables. All three aircraft in the section kept formation right until the Rhine came into view, when it was found to everyone's alarm that Gibson's Lancaster, leading the whole flight, was no less than six miles too far to the south and heading for Duisburg, one of the most heavily defended towns in the whole Ruhr. He made a sharp turn to remedy the potential danger of the situation and flew along the line of the Rhine, under heavy fire from barges on the river equipped with quick-firing weapons.

On to the Ruhr Valley, with half an hour to go before the Mohne Dam. Ceaseless anti-aircraft fire forced Gibson to take evasive action. The three were also being continually caught by searchlights, some of which Gibson managed to avoid by 'dodging behind trees', as he put it.

Then they flew over a new and heavily defended airfield near Dorsten, not marked on their maps, where all three were held by searchlights. Gibson's rear-gunner fired at the beams but stopped when some tall trees came between the lights and the aircraft. Suddenly the searchlights were extinguished by a long burst from the rear turret of one of the other two Lancasters.

It was about here that one of the aircraft of the first wave of nine was lost. Gibson sent a radio warning of this new airfield to following aircraft. Lancasters B, N and Z formed the second section. Shortly before it was lost, aircraft B broke formation, presumably for the pilot to check his position. The pilot of Lancaster N, then flying at 100 feet, reported that soon afterwards he saw a bomber being shot at by anti-aircraft guns and returning their fire. Then he saw an explosion on the ground. The inference was that Lancaster B had crashed, its mine probably exploding at the same time. The other eight Lancasters flew on, past Dortmund and Hamm, avoiding more fire from the ground. Then hills rose ahead, and open country apparently without defences. Gibson gained height to get over a hill and then saw the Mohne Dam lake ahead – and in a moment the dam itself. From all along the dam, which looked, Gibson said, rather like a battleship, guns were firing, as well as from a powerhouse below the dam; but there were no searchlights. Gibson estimated that tracer was coming from five positions, and probably a dozen guns in all. They all circled around getting their bearings, and each time one of them came within range of the guns on the dam they received accurate fire. One of the eight aircraft was hit, but not fatally.

Gibson first in

Although the attack on the Sorpe Dam had been planned for this precise time, as an effective diversion from the efforts of the main force of Lancasters against the Mohne, only one of the five aircraft aiming for the Sorpe Dam had in fact reached it. They had met heavy opposition early on. Lancaster K and E had both been shot down near the Dutch coast; H had hit the sea and lost its mine in the process, so had returned to base; W had been hit by flak which disrupted the intercom, so that the pilot had had to return home. Only Lancaster T attacked the Sorpe Dam, a minute or two before 3 a.m. on 17 May.

Back at the Mohne Dam, the Lancasters had scattered, ready for the attack. Gibson was due in first. He made a wide circle, and then came down over the hills at the eastern end of the Mohne lake. He dived towards the water and flew at exactly sixty feet, with the spotlights meeting on the water below. With these lights on, the bomber made a still simpler target for the gunners on the dam, who could see it coming from more than two miles away. Tracer shells converged towards it as Gibson flew straight and level towards the dam. The bomber's gunners replied. Gibson said afterwards that he expected to die at any moment. But the Lancaster was not hit anywhere. The mine was released, and Gibson flew in a circle.

Looking back at the lake, the crew saw a fountain of water, white in the late moonlight, and 1,000 feet high. The surface of the lake had been broken, and sheets of water were pouring over the dam. At first Gibson thought it had burst at the initial attempt, but he soon realized that it was only water churned up by the explosion. The mine had gone off five yards from the dam, but Gibson had to signal home that there was no apparent breach. Back in England, 'Bomber' Harris, Barnes Wallis and the rest received the news breathlessly, and waited for the next report. They had to hang on for fully thirteen minutes.

Gibson waited for the water to subside, and then signalled to Lancaster M to make its attack. The same thing happened all over again. The enemy guns focused on the lone bomber. Some 100 yards from the dam, a jet of flame sprang from the aircraft. Gibson inferred that the bomb-aimer had been wounded because the mine fell late and onto the powerhouse below.

The pilot was striving desperately to gain height for his crew to bail out of the blazing bomber. He got up to 500 feet, and then there was a flash in the sky, and one wing fell off. The whole aircraft came apart in the air, and fell to the ground in fragments. Almost immediately afterwards, the mine that had fallen on the powerhouse exploded. This caused so much smoke that Gibson had to wait some minutes for it to clear before he could direct the next aircraft to attack.

For this third attempt Guy Gibson had a plan. As Lancaster P flew towards the dam Gibson went alongside, a little ahead of it, and then turned. His rear gunner fired at the flak positions on the dam, and at the same time helped to draw off their fire from the bomber about to attack the dam.

Lancaster P was hit several times despite Gibson's help, and all the petrol drained from one of the wing tanks, but the mine was accurately released and exploded fifty yards from the dam. Again, circling near the scene Gibson thought he saw some movement of the wall, but although the same huge fountain of water was thrust up, it was clear that the dam had not yet been breached.

Now it came to Lancaster A's turn. Gibson developed his diversionary tactics still further this time, and as the bomber began its run in towards the dam Gibson flew up and down on the farther side of the dam and ordered his gunners to fire on the enemy's positions. To make sure that they would concentrate on him rather than Lancaster A Gibson had his identification lights switched on. The plan was successful, and the enemy did in fact keep their guns trained on his Lancaster while the attacking one flew straight towards the dam. As the mine exploded a huge wave went over the dam, but although it had gone off in contact with the wall they were still unable to report any apparent breach. Back at headquarters

the tension was becoming increasingly unbearable, as each attack failed to bring about the desired effect.

Gibson ordered Lancaster J to attack. The fifth mine went up almost exactly in the correct spot. Just before the moment of release, however, the pilot reported seeing a breach in the centre. The bomber's own mine flung up the usual fantastic fountain, and then the aircraft became badly harried by enemy gunfire. Gibson himself could not see the dam at that moment, so was in no position to confirm a breach. He knew that time was running out, however, so decided to send the next bomber into the attack. Just as he had ordered Lancaster L to start, he turned and came close to the wall of the dam. But it had rolled over. Quickly he told Lancaster L to turn away. Gibson flew close and looked again. Then he saw plainly that there was a breach in the dam 150 yards wide. A huge cataract of water was churning through the breach. At 12.56 a.m. Gibson signalled to group headquarters the prearranged code-word 'Nigger', meaning that the Mohne Dam had been breached. Nigger, his dog, had been run over and killed the evening of the day before the attack.

An unbelievable wave

The valley below the dam was filling with fog, evaporating from the water that was pouring down it. It was moving in an unbelievable wave, and in front of this Gibson could see the headlights of cars racing to safety. The headlights changed colour, first to green, and then eventually to dark purple, as the water overtook them. The water surged on towards the eastern end of the Ruhr Valley. The powerhouse beside the dam was by now completely submerged.

Gibson circled for three minutes and then called up the rest of his force. He ordered aircraft J and P to make for home. Lancaster M had been shot down. The rest of the force Gibson ordered to set course for the Eder Dam. Gibson's own G and Lancaster A no longer had their mines, but they went as well; L, Z and N still carried their mines intact.

It was getting late by the time they all reached the Eder Dam, which lay in a deep valley among wooded hills, and at the far end of the lake was a hill about 1,000 feet high with a castle on top of it. They had to approach the dam by flying over this hill, and then diving steeply from above the castle, down to sixty feet over the water. Lancaster L made three runs before the bomb-aimer released the mine. A great spurt of water was followed by a small gap towards the east side of the dam. Next followed Z, after two attempts. Gibson saw a vivid explosion on the parapet of the dam itself, which lit up the whole valley. Then no more was seen of the Lancaster, which must have been blown up by its own mine on the parapet.

At 1.52 a.m. Lancaster N attacked, successfully this time. A cone of water rose up, then a thirty-foot breach appeared below the top of the dam, leaving the top intact for a moment. A torrent of water cascaded downwards and rushed in a tidal wave to the valley below. Gibson's wireless operator signalled the code-word 'Dinghy'. The Eder Dam had been breached, too.

So the five aircraft set course for home, with the enemy's fighter force now fully aroused. Lancaster A failed to return. Some time on the way back, Gibson's rear gunner warned him that there was an enemy aircraft behind. Gibson lost height, though he was already flying very low, and made towards the west, where the sky was darkest; by this manoeuvre he evaded the enemy.

One of the reserve managed to get through to attack the Sorpe Dam at 3.14 a.m.

Eight of the Lancasters making this historic raid were lost. But without Guy Gibson's own heroism, both at Mohne and Eder, in drawing enemy fire on his own Lancaster, the losses would have been even heavier.

There is scarcely need to repeat the chaos caused by the raid. Headlines have told the story before:

'Growing devastation in the Ruhr.'
'Flood waters sweep into Kassel.'
'Damage to German war industries.'
'Dam floods stretch for sixty miles.'

On 19 September 1944, Guy Gibson, master bomber, led one last raid on Rheydt, in the Rhineland, a strongly defended rail centre and traffic terminus for the Ruhr. He was flying below the main force, guiding the bombing, talking to his fellow pilots, telling them where and when to strike.

Over the target, his Lancasters coming in to bomb high above him heard his characteristic voice on the radio-telephone, calm, unhurried. His instructions came clearly, and they followed them carefully. The bombs hit an ammunition train and started a series of fires and explosions. The crews heard his final orders.

His aircraft crashed near Bergen-op-Zoom, on the East Scheldt estuary, where his body was found and buried.

The U-Boat War

Catalina, Liberator, Sunderland and Flying Fortress

The aeroplane was one of the submarine's deadliest enemies, and the running battle which Coastal Command waged against the German U-boats was of incalculable assistance to the vital Atlantic convoys. At first Coastal Command seemed to be getting the upper hand, but then the U-boats began hunting in packs – 'wolf packs' – and were fitted with new, heavier anti-aircraft guns. No longer did the U-boat commanders order an urgent dive when a Liberator or other bomber was sighted. Instead the vessels stayed on the surface and could put up such a strong barrage that the attacking aircraft stood a substantial chance of being hit if not shot down.

Unless the air crews showed a high order of heroism, all the scientific aids they possessed, such as advanced depth charges and other anti-submarine projectiles, would be useless. There was nothing for it but to 'fly down the barrels of the U-boat guns' – not a pleasant assignment, even in fast aeroplanes. But these crews had to handle heavy cumbersome flying boats or bombers, designed to operate from high altitudes. Moreover, these air attacks inevitably occurred several hundred miles out to sea, where rescue was rare. The result would often be the exchange of an aircraft for a submarine. And yet the air crews did not complain. They accepted the new strategy of the enemy and set about beating him at it.

The submarines obstinately stayed on the surface, hoping to deter the Allied airmen from attacking. But they were not to be put off. Time and time again one aircraft would dive down on a pack of the enemy and thunder right into the convergent shells. Often the aircraft scored successes. Just as often the Germans got the aircraft as well. The crews just hoped to survive somehow. Some did, others did not.

For instance, Wing Commander R. B. Thompson, captaining an R.A.F. Fortress, was lucky. They sank the U-boat but crashed into the sea beside the wreckage of the vessel they had just destroyed. They managed to get themselves and a dinghy clear of the Fortress, and then set about staying afloat and alive. Thompson and his crew drifted for four days and nights before they were rescued. Flying Officer A. A. Bishop in a Royal Canadian Air Force Sunderland flying boat forced his attack home on a U-boat and sank it. But the front turret of the flying boat was half shot away before the U-boat finally went down. The wings, galley and bomb-bay were all blazing badly, and the flying boat had to crash-land on the sea. The end of this particular episode was also happy: the survivors of both the Sunderland and the U-boat were picked up sodden and shivering by a British destroyer.

Liberator versus U-boat

Flying Officer Lloyd Trigg had rendered outstanding service on convoy escort and anti-U-boat duties. He had completed forty-six sorties. On 11 August 1943 he undertook a patrol in a Liberator bomber as captain and pilot, although he had not previously made any operational sorties in this type of aircraft. No. 200 Squadron had only recently switched over from Hudsons to Liberators.

Trigg took off with a crew of four fellow New Zealanders and two Englishmen. They left the airfield of Yundum, near Bathhurst, West Africa, and set course westwards, to an area where several Coastal Command bombers and flying boats had recently been shot down. Hour after hour the Liberator flew back and forth, covering the sea where the U-boats were most expected.

After eight hours' flying they spotted a U-boat on the surface, fitted with the latest large-bore anti-aircraft guns. Trigg prepared to attack at once. He nosed the Liberator down to be sure of getting into a good position, but in so doing the aircraft met the full focus of these new weapons, especially the forward gun. Trigg made his first run right across the U-boat. Then he wheeled round and came in again. Bombs burst on each flank of the vessel, spuming water over her. The Liberator received many hits. Fire broke out, and a further hit after the second run caught its tail. Flames engulfed the tail rapidly.

This was the critical moment for Trigg. He had to decide whether to break off the attack and try to make a forced landing on the sea. All question was already past of keeping the Liberator airborne to fly back to base. If Trigg continued the engagement, the Liberator would offer a 'no-deflection' target to the anti-aircraft fire, while every second spent in the air would increase the extent and intensity of the flames now coursing

inside and out. The decision to continue would also obviously diminish the chances of survival of himself and his crew.

Without hesitation Trigg maintained their course, in spite of the precarious condition of the aircraft, and proceeded to carry out a masterly attack on the already smouldering U-boat. Skimming over the water at less than fifty feet, with anti-aircraft fire entering his open bomb doors, he dropped his bombs on and around the U-boat, where they exploded with undoubted effect. The Liberator limped clear of the vessel and a little way farther on it dived into the sea, taking Trigg and his crew with it.

But the U-boat was already doomed. In twenty minutes it sank. Some of her crew struggled through the water to swim clear of their vessel and towards the wreckage of the Liberator. They saw the bomber's rubber dinghy, which had broken loose, and got aboard it. When the Germans were rescued two days later by the corvette H.M.S. *Clarkia* they told the story of the attack and their own subsequent ordeal.

On its third attack the Liberator was hit full and square by a shell, but continuing on its course it dropped its bombs near the hull of the submarine, damaging the vessel so severely that the batteries began to release chlorine gas. The aircraft flew on at over 200 miles an hour, hit the sea, and sank in a few seconds.

Half the German crew were overcome by gas, but twenty-four survivors were left in the water when the U-boat sank. One particular German sighted the Liberator's rubber dinghy, and it was he who reached it half an hour after the U-boat disappeared. He then paddled in the direction of his companions. But only six men, including the captain, were able to reach the dinghy, and although they paddled round the spot for a long time they found no further trace of their companions.

Next day an R.A.F. aircraft circled them and dropped supplies. At that time the Germans were thought to be survivors of the Liberator, for which a search had been made as soon as it had been posted overdue. When the *Clarkia* finally found the U-boat survivors, the Germans were generous in their praise of the captain and crew of the Liberator, for the daring and courage which had brought them victory at the cost of their lives. Lloyd Trigg and his crew were 'expendable' in the Battle of the Atlantic, but without them and all the other Coastal Command crews it could not have been won.

Another example was Flying Officer John 'Joe' Cruickshank, who was struck in seventy-two places by pieces of flak while piloting a Catalina flying boat. It seems incredible that a man could survive such injuries.

A staunch-looking Scot with a dark moustache, Cruickshank started flying with Coastal Command early in 1943. On 17 July 1944 he was piloting his Catalina between sixty-nine and seventy degrees north-west of the Lofoten Islands on a normal anti-submarine patrol, when his navigator operating the radar roused him with a shout of 'Blip up, about sixteen miles away'. They were now inside the Arctic Circle, no place to be ditched even in midsummer.

The Catalina flew towards the spot, and then slightly to starboard the crew saw the tell-tale plume of foam. The submarine surfaced: one of the latest type of U-boat with a tonnage five times as great as the standard model. From his pilot's seat, Cruickshank could see 37 mm and 20 mm anti-aircraft cannon behind the conning tower. He took his aircraft in to attack, flying into the wind so that his engine noise would be carried away from the U-boat. There was not a sign that they had been spotted. The bomb-aimer's thumb stabbed the release button, but nothing happened. The depth charge had jammed. A double danger at once, from the U-boat and from their own weapon!

By now they had been seen. The enemy guns blasted the air around them. Levelling up at fifty feet above the Arctic, Cruickshank began a turn for another run. He had no thought of giving up at that stage. Within seconds the shells were punctuating the airspace near the cumbersome Catalina as she made her turn. He banked heavily.

'Hold on, we're going back,' he shouted into the mouthpiece of his intercom. It was his twenty-fifth Coastal Command patrol and the first time he had sighted a U-boat. He began his second turn over the vessel. The whole armoury belched up as they came down to depth charge-dropping height – right in the teeth of the cannon. The shells could hardly have missed them.

Dickson, the navigator bomb-aimer, was killed outright. The twenty-year-old wireless operator, Flight Sergeant John Appleton, described what happened next: 'The skipper called "Everybody ready?" and then "In we go again." We made a perfect run-in at low level. When almost on top of the U-boat another shell burst in the aircraft. Everything seemed to happen in a flash. I was hit in my head and hands. Cruickshank took no notice. He continued straight on.'

There were explosions in the Catalina, and the second pilot and two others of the crew fell injured. The nose gunner had his leg riddled with scalding shrapnel. Fire broke out, and the aircraft filled with the fumes of exploding shells. The whole frame of the aircraft was devastated.

Cruickshank was hit in seventy-two places, by seventy-two separate pieces of flak. He received two serious wounds in the lungs and ten penetrations in the lower limbs. But he did not falter. He flew the Catalina right over the enemy, released the depth charges himself, and straddled the submarine perfectly. A gunner fought the flames with an extinguisher all the time Cruickshank was making his attack. The U-boat sank, vanishing in a soap-flake froth.

But the fire was still burning. At this moment Cruickshank collapsed and the second pilot took over the controls. He was Flight Sergeant Jack Garnett, and though himself wounded he managed to steady the Catalina sufficiently to keep it airborne. Soon afterwards, Cruickshank came round again, and although he was bleeding profusely he insisted on resuming command and taking over the controls. He did take over and retained his hold until he was satisfied that the damaged aircraft could be kept under control, that they had set a course for base, and that all the necessary signals had been sent. Only after all this could Garnett persuade him to accept medical aid. Despite the seventy-two wounds, he refused morphia in case it prevented him from carrying on if he was needed.

Could he survive?

Then came the long run home. The attack had been made at almost maximum distance from base. Now the two main questions were: could the Catalina keep going, and could Cruickshank live long enough to get back for proper medical attention?

They carried him aft and put him on the only serviceable bunk. The others had been on fire. Fortunately, all the fires were got under control fairly soon. Wireless Operator Appleton dressed his wounds and they kept him warm with their Irvin jackets. He recovered again and asked for something to drink and a cigarette. He was very thirsty. He kept asking if everything was all right, and insisted on periodic checks.

As the hours passed, they left the Lofotens behind and headed for the Shetlands. Several times Cruickshank lapsed into unconsciousness, and he lost a lot of blood. Yet when he came round each time, his first thought was for the safety of the aircraft and crew. It still seemed touch and go whether he could last out till they reached the Shetlands.

The hobbling Catalina flew right through the evening till about 10 p.m., double British summer time. It was dusk, and the Shetlands were dimmed. Cruickshank rallied enough to realize that with the aircraft in its present condition they would have to take great care in bringing her down on the water, especially since the second pilot had also been injured. He could only breathe now with agony, but he insisted on being carried forward and propped up in the second pilot's seat. Somehow he stayed conscious.

Sullom Voe lay below now; they had only to get down. But Cruickshank refused to let them rush it. For a full hour he gave orders as they were needed. He would not bring down the Catalina until the conditions of light and sea made it possible with the minimum of risk. With his help the Catalina eventually landed on the friendly waters off Sullom Voe. Even then Cruickshank directed it while they taxied across the bay and beached, so that it could be easily salvaged.

The base had received their signals and a medical officer was waiting to go on board as soon as the big flying boat ground to a stop on the shingle of the Shetlands. As it did so, Cruickshank collapsed. He should have done so hours earlier; only indomitable will-power had kept him going. The medical officer gave him a blood transfusion on the spot, and life flowed slowly back again. Then they removed him gently to hospital, where he had to remain for several months before he was well again – which is not surprising in view of the number of his wounds. The surprising thing was that he survived at all.

Nuremberg and Schweinfurt

Halifax and Lancaster

On 30 March 1944 no fewer than ninety-six bombers were reported missing from the night's raid on Germany. It was one of the Allies' heaviest losses in a bomber raid.

Cyril Barton was captain and pilot of a Halifax bomber detailed to attack Nuremberg. Seventy miles short of the target, a Ju 88 swooped on the aircraft. The very first burst of fire from it put the entire intercom system right out of action. An Me 210 joined in and damaged one engine. The bomber's machine guns went out of action, so the gunners could not return the German fighter's fire.

Somehow Barton managed to keep his Halifax on course, covering those seventy miles to Nuremberg, although fighters continued to attack him all the way to the target area. But in the confusion caused by the failure of the intercom system at the height of the battle, a signal had been misinterpreted, and the navigator, air bomber and wireless operator had all left the aircraft by parachute.

Barton then faced a situation of dire peril. His aircraft was damaged, his navigational team had gone, and he could not communicate with the rest of the crew. If he continued his mission he could be at the mercy of hostile fighters, when silhouetted against the fires in the target area; and if he happened to survive that, he would have to make a four and a half hour journey home on three engines across heavily defended enemy territory. Barton determined to press on, however; he reached his target, and released the bombs himself.

As he wrenched the Halifax round to aim for home, the propeller of the damaged engine, which had been vibrating badly, flew off. Two of the bomber's petrol tanks had also suffered damage and were leaking. But Barton remained aloof from all these dangers and concentrated on the task of holding to his course without any navigational aids and against strong headwinds. Somehow he successfully avoided the most strongly defended areas on his return route.

Using just his own judgment, he eventually crossed the English coast only ninety miles north of his base. Now the worst part was about to begin. As a result of the leaks in the petrol tanks, fuel was nearly non-existent. The port engines stopped with a sickening, intermittent cough. Seeing a suitable landing place – for the aircraft was now too low to be abandoned successfully – Barton ordered the three remaining members of the Halifax crew to take up crash stations. The bomber lost height rapidly. With only one engine functioning, he struggled to land clear of a group of houses just below them. The three members of the crew survived, but Barton was killed in the crash. The three who bailed out over Germany were safe too, as prisoners-of-war, so he alone died, while the other six survived.

Mrs Barton read the letter Cyril had written in case this ever happened:

Dear Mum,

I hope you never receive this, but I quite expect you will. I'm expecting to do my first operational trip in a few days. I know what ops over Germany mean, and I have no illusions about it. By my own calculations the average life of a crew is 20 ops, and we have 30 to do in our first tour.

I'm writing this for two reasons. One to tell you how I would like my money spent that I have left behind me; two to tell you how I feel about meeting my Maker.

1. I intended as you know, taking a university course with my savings. Well, I would like it to be spent over the education of my brothers and sisters.

2. All I can say about this is that I am quite prepared to die. It holds no terror for me.

At times I've wondered whether I've been right in believing what I do, and just recently I've doubted the veracity of the Bible, but in the little time I've had to sort out intellectual problems I've been left with a bias in favour of the Bible.

Apart from this, though, I have the inner conviction as I write, of a force outside myself, and my brain tells me that I have not trusted in vain. All I am anxious about is that you and the rest of the family will also come to know Him. Ken, I know, already does. I commend my Saviour to you.

I am writing to Doreen separately. I expect you will have guessed by now that we are quite in love with each other.

Well, that's covered everything now I guess, so love to Dad and all,
Your loving son
CYRIL

Cyril Barton was awarded the Victoria Cross.

Fire at 20,000 feet

Four weeks later, Norman Jackson became the first R.A.F. flight engineer to win the V.C. D-Day was approaching. On the morning of 26 April 1944 Jackson got a telegram telling him of the birth of a son. He and the rest of the Lancaster crew were jubilant and excited about this – especially since the night's operation against Schweinfurt was due to be the last of his Bomber Command tour. He had already completed a Coastal Command tour. Once the night of 26

April was over, that would be two tours over as well.

Despite the expected opposition, they had a reasonable approach to their target of Schweinfurt and dropped their bombs successfully. The Lancaster had climbed out of the inferno of the target area and reached 20,000 feet when an enemy fighter pounced on it. The captain reacted instinctively and took evasive action, but the fighter secured several hits on the four-engine bomber. Fire broke out near a petrol tank on the upper surface of the starboard wing, between the fuselage and the inner engine.

The evasive tactics during the engagement had thrown Jackson to the floor, where he sustained a series of wounds from shell splinters in the right leg and shoulder. He recovered himself quickly, and got the captain's permission to try and put out the flames. He knew they could not fly back to England in that state; indeed that they could not fly for long at all unless something were done.

Stuffing a hand fire-extinguisher into the top of his life-saving jacket, and clipping on his parachute pack, Jackson jettisoned the escape hatch above the pilot's head. Then he started to climb out of the cockpit and back along the top of the fuselage to the starboard wing. But before he could leave the fuselage his parachute pack opened, and the whole canopy and rigging lines streamed and spilled into the cockpit.

Undeterred, he went on. The pilot, bomb-aimer and navigator gathered the parachute together, paying them out as the sergeant climbed aft; all this still four miles high above hostile country. Eventually Jackson slipped, but falling from the fuselage to the starboard wing he somehow grasped an air intake on the leading edge of the wing. Every sinew strained beyond the normal limits, he succeeded in clinging on, but inevitably lost the extinguisher, which was sucked away with the piercing windstream.

By this time the fire had spread alarmingly, and continued to do so progressively. Jackson himself became involved in it. His face, hands and clothes were severely burned. Charred and in pain, he could not keep his hold, and was swept through the flames and over the trailing edge of the wing. When the rest of the crew glimpsed him he was dragging his parachute behind him. It was only partly inflated, and burning in a number of places.

The captain realized that the fire could not possibly be controlled now, and gave the order to abandon ship. Four members of the crew bailed out safely, and were taken prisoner, but the captain and rear gunner failed to get out. So

Flying Officer Fred Mifflin and Flight Sergeant Hugh Johnson died as the blazing Lancaster crashed.

Meanwhile the wind gasped through the nylon and the lines of Jackson's parachute, spreading the patches of fire as he fell. His speed increased. Jackson could not control his descent at all, but thankfully it did not reach a fatal rate. He landed heavily, breaking his ankle; so with this, his right eye closed through burns, other burns hurting him, and his hands useless, he could only wait for daybreak, when he crawled to the nearest village. He rapped on the door of the smallest cottage he could see, and an old woman and her daughter gave him first aid. Then, after rough medical treatment at a nearby hospital, he was paraded through the village. People turned out to jeer and throw stones at him, but he was too far gone to care.

He was made a prisoner-of-war and there followed ten months in hospital, where he made a good recovery. But long before all this the whole crew had been posted as missing. Two and a half weeks went by before German radio announced that Jackson was a prisoner-of-war with the four others.

All that remained in 1945 was for them to be returned home soon after V.E. Day, when it was found that his hands needed still further treatment, and were only of limited use to him. It was at this stage that the whole story was pieced together by the reports of the rest of the crew: how he had ventured out of the Lancaster at a great height and in intense cold; how he had ignored the extra hazard of his spilled parachute, and how, if he had managed to subdue the flames, there would have been little or no prospect of his getting back into the cockpit.

After this 'almost incredible feat', as it was officially called, Jackson was awarded the Victoria Cross on 26 October 1945. The day after the announcement, he was looking for a house for his wife and baby son Brian, who had been born the day before the raid on Schweinfurt. They did find a bungalow eventually, in Burton's Road, Hampton Hill, Middlesex. Outside it at night passers-by could see the silhouette of a Lancaster lit up in a porthole-shaped window. There was no need to ask Jackson what it meant or why he put it there.

The Pathfinders

Lancaster and Mosquito

In October 1943 Leonard Cheshire took command of 617 Squadron and opened his fourth operational tour as a wing commander. He had relinquished the rank of group captain at his own request to take up flying duties again. He was already one of the most decorated men in the Royal Air Force.

He soon began to devise a fresh way of ensuring accuracy against comparatively small targets. It developed as the new marking system by an aircraft flying lower than the rest of the force, and Cheshire pioneered this 'master bomber' technique with 617 Squadron, confirming its effect in practice by attacks on the flying bomb sites in the Pas de Calais. The method was later adopted for a series of small specialized raids on targets in France vitally associated with German aircraft production. By the end of March 1944 eleven of these twelve targets had been destroyed or damaged, using the new marker system of attack and a 12,000-pound blast-bomb.

The very first raid with this remarkable bomb was on an aero-engine factory at Limoges on 8 February. Cheshire led twelve Lancasters through cloud to reach the target in moonlight. He then dipped his marker Lancaster down to a mere 200 feet over the factory and dropped a load of incendiaries right in the middle of it. These burst at once, throwing up volumes of smoke. The deputy leader then dropped two red-spot fires from 7,000 feet into the incendiaries, so the rest of the bombers had a perfect aiming point. Four of the five 12,000-pound monsters fell right on the factory, all four obtaining direct hits on separate buildings. The damage was therefore quite devastating.

Cheshire soon realized that something more manoeuvrable than a Lancaster was needed for the marker, and so got two Mosquitoes for this low-level task.

The 'master bomber' technique quickly established itself as adaptable to all conditions, where more normal methods would have failed. On 10 March the squadron target was a needle bearing factory comprising an area only 170 by 90 yards. Despite the weather forecast of a full moon and clear visibility, a screen of cloud obscured practically all the moonlight. Cheshire and his deputy tried repeatedly to pick out and mark the target but decided it was no good using the red-spot fires or green indicators as intended. Improvising immediately, Cheshire dropped incendiaries on the eastern and western edges of the target, and then told the force to bomb between these twin glows. Although their success seemed doubtful, later daylight reconnaissance proved that they had succeeded beyond all their expectations, and almost entirely destroyed the vital small factory.

Still operating over France, one of Cheshire's next targets called for bombing on an altogether larger scale: the railway marshalling yards at La Chappelle, just north of Paris. The night of 20–21 April was chosen for the attack, as part of the general pre-invasion softening up and dislocation of communications in the entire northern France region. 617 Squadron was only one of many participating, and the plan called for separate attacks on two aiming points within the overall target of the marshalling yards. More than 250 aircraft were to be employed.

Bombing had developed by now into a highly skilful and scientific operation. First of all, at 12.03 a.m., six Mosquitoes reached the target area two minutes ahead of the time for the start of the attack. These aircraft dropped window – strips of metal-covered paper – to confuse the enemy's radar-directed air and ground defences.

Aircraft from a group other than Cheshire's were due to drop green target indicators first of all, but although these devices were released they failed to cascade at once, so little time remained for Cheshire to find and mark the exact bombing point. He operated rapidly, however, and located the aiming point, marking it with red-spot fires, and telling his deputy to add more fires for a clearer indication. He gave orders for the controller of the force to instruct bombing to begin, but a further delay occurred due to a failure in the V.H.F. radio-telephone between Cheshire and the controller, who did not receive the instructions till after the main force of bombers was actually in the La Chappelle area. Despite the delay and congestion, the attack proceeded smoothly from then on, and subsequent reconnaissance revealed that the entire zone around the aiming point lay utterly irreparable. This yielded further proof of the efficacy of the marker technique, which had survived even

setbacks such as the delay of the first indicators to cascade and the interruption of communication between Cheshire and the attack controller.

Much of the Allied bombing potential was naturally being directed against the invasion areas and the links with it, but Cheshire and his squadron fulfilled a wish to try out the marker technique where it would be most severely tested: against targets in Germany itself. Two raids during April especially proved its worth, the first on Brunswick, the second on Munich.

Cheshire's group, No. 5, received orders to bomb Brunswick on 22 April with a strong force, which turned out to be 265 aircraft. Two Mosquitoes went ahead to report on the weather to the twenty Lancasters due to mark the target: the industrial region of Brunswick. But trouble developed with their V.H.F. radio-telephones, so no such reports were returned. The next confusion came when the enemy – wise to the new flare system – began laying their own dummy target indicators. They looked like the genuine article, but unluckily for the Germans were the wrong colour! The lack of contact with the two Mosquitoes, however, was one of the things which caused the first of the flare force to drop its flares in the wrong area by about five miles.

The error did not prove too serious though, for the ever-alert Cheshire made a low-level reconnaissance by the light they had created, and realized the mistake. He did not release his vital markers yet, waiting for another batch of flares to go down. This shot was much more on the mark, and by their light the aiming point could be assessed as accurately as necessary.

With the right region marked by the familiar red-spot fires, Cheshire authorized the attack to begin. But all did not go smoothly, because of the difficulty in the V.H.F. communication. The interference on the V.H.F. resulted in orders being partly misinterpreted, so that some of the crews bombed the German dummy green target indicators instead of the accurately placed red-spot fires. Cheshire had to report that only half the bombs of the main force fell in the target area, the rest exploding in the wrong area that had been illuminated by green indicators. Nevertheless, a railway equipment works, an artillery tractor plant and other industrial objectives were struck by at least fifty per cent of the 741 tons dropped during the operation. Only three of the 265 aircraft were lost – a remarkably low proportion for a raid so deep into Germany.

Directly after Brunswick followed the famous Munich raid. Munich was selected for this attack so that the method of marking at low level could be tested against a heavily defended target in the heart of the Reich: Munich had particularly fierce anti-aircraft and search-light defences. The number of guns in the immediate area of Munich was thought to be 200: nearly one for each aircraft.

It was only two nights after the Brunswick bombing, on 24 April, that exactly the same number of aircraft aimed for the city so dear to Hitler and the Nazi movement. All except ten of these actually attacked. The scientific approach reached one sophisticated stage further with the inclusion of a feint raid on Milan by half a dozen Lancasters of 617 Squadron to lure enemy fighters from Munich.

The operation is described by W. J. Lawrence in his book *No. 5 Bomber Group RAF*:

'In order that as little as possible of the route for the main force should be over Germany, the force flew towards the south-west of France, as far southwards as Lake Annecy. By this lake, and at a farther position some distance to the north-east, long-burning red target indicators were dropped to serve as route markers, and the second of these two positions was also appointed as a rendezvous for the force; all crews of the main force were instructed not to leave the rendezvous until a given time, in order that they might reach the target in a compact stream.

But eleven Mosquitoes of 627 Squadron flew by a much more direct route to release Window for 2½ minutes before the first flares were to be dropped, and then to carry out a dive-bombing attack.

Four Mosquitoes, flown by Wing Commander Cheshire, Squadron Leader Shannon, and Flight Lieutenants Kearns and Fawke, which were to carry out the first marking of the target, also flew by a direct route; this involved flying over the defences of Augsburg, and from there until Munich the aircraft had to pass through continuous anti-aircraft fire. They arrived punctually at the moment when the first flares were dropped.

As he reached the target, Wing Commander Cheshire was caught in a cone of many searchlights, and as flares were then being dropped by Lancasters flying far above him, his aircraft was lit up both from above and from below. Every gun within range opened fire on him. He dived to 700 feet, and from that height identified the aiming point and dropped red-spot fires accurately on it at 1.41 a.m.

He ordered the three Mosquitoes accompanying him to back up these first markers, and this was done; the main force began bombing and Lancasters of No. 617 Squadron continued to reinforce the original red-spot fires with others, in order that the aiming point might be continuously marked.

Aircraft of the main force were then flying at the same height as the marking Lancasters, and as a result one of these marking Lancasters had to make a second run, only to have to swerve again at the last moment to avoid a collision, with the result that its red-spot fires fell about 500 yards to the east of the aiming point; at about the same time a target indicator which seemed to be an enemy decoy fell some distance to the west of the aiming point. The controller, and leader for the flare force, Wing Commander Dean, then ordered the green target indicators to be dropped on the aiming point by aircraft of the flare force to back up the correctly placed red-spot fires, and this appears to have been an effective measure; there was, however, some tendency for the bombing to spread in the later stages of the attack as the aiming point became obscured by smoke and the glare of incendiaries.

Wing Commander Cheshire continued to fly over the city at a height of about 1,000 feet in the earlier stages of the attack, and as the bombs were falling, his aircraft was hit and damaged by shell fragments, but he continued to direct the operation. At one moment he was so blinded by the glare of searchlights that he almost lost control of his aircraft. When eventually he was satisfied that he could do no more, he set course for base, but found it even more difficult and dangerous to disengage himself from the defences than it had been to approach the target; even after leaving the centre of the city he was under withering fire for fully twelve minutes before he got clear.

Other marker aircraft were coned by searchlights, which extended in a great belt, for about fifty miles after they had left the target. Several combats were seen to take place over Munich itself, and four aircraft were seen to be shot down in the target area. Nine aircraft were missing, roughly 3.5 per cent of the whole force dispatched.'

The damage done was out of all proportion to the size of the force, and much of Munich seemed affected, including Nazi buildings.

To Leonard Cheshire, the final weeks before

the invasion meant more operations with his marker method. During his fourth tour of duty, he led 617 Squadron on every occasion.

One such operation early in May 1944 was against the large military depot and tank park at Mailly-le-Camp, where thousands of enemy troops were believed to be located. Cheshire's Mosquito hummed over the area in dazzlingly clear moonlight, but despite the fact that this was the only operation of the night, so that all enemy fighters could be made available against the attack, he managed to mark the target correctly. The attack went ahead as planned, but because of the bright moonlight and the quantity of fighters available against them, forty-two bombers were lost out of the 338 that set out from England. But the effects of the raid offset these losses.

Contribution to D-Day

As his contribution to D-Day, Cheshire led Operation Taxable. This was designed to mislead the enemy radar defences between Dover and Cap d'Antifer into thinking that an armada was approaching that part of the coast.

Sixteen Lancasters and eighteen small ships were chosen to create this illusion. Some of the ships towed balloons with reflectors attached, to simulate the sort of radar echoes emitted by large ships. The Lancasters had the more unusual job though. They had to stooge around at precise points in flattened ellipses and release window.

Cheshire said: 'The tactics were to use two formations of aircraft with the rear formation seven miles behind the leaders, each aircraft being separated laterally by two miles. Individual aircraft flew a straight course of seven miles, turned round and flew on the reciprocal one mile away. On completion of the second leg, it returned to its former course and repeated the procedure over again, advancing far enough to keep in line with the convoy's speed of seven knots.'

An average of two bundles of window were jettisoned on each circuit. The operation started soon after dusk on D−1 and went on steadily until the D-Day landings along the Normandy coast. It played a valuable part in helping to achieve surprise for the greatest invasion in history.

So D-Day came and went. And with it came a new weapon to 617 Squadron, even bigger than the blast-bomb. This was the terrifying 'Tallboy', a 14,000-pounder which reached the ground at a speed faster than that of sound – so no warning preceded its arrival. It was developed for targets

where the deepest penetration was needed, and extreme accuracy would be essential.

Tallboy made its debut on 8 June, when 617 Squadron attacked the Saumur railway tunnel, which ran north-east to the Normandy front. Four Lancasters of another squadron were detailed to drop flares, so that Cheshire could lead the assault by marking the target. This small flare force encountered difficulty, yet although many flares dropped wide Cheshire could make out his whereabouts just sufficiently to release his red-spot fires into the cutting leading to the tunnel, only forty yards from its actual mouth. Nineteen Lancasters made the attack with Tallboys after several dummy runs to be sure they were in the precise position. Here they had to be exact, but it could hardly be expected that many of their giant bombs would drop in so small an area.

In fact, one fell on the roof of the tunnel, the crater caused by this being 100 feet wide, and three exploded in the deep cutting approaching the Saumur tunnel, blocking the whole railway with craters still wider than the one on the roof. And the main line stayed blocked until the Allied armies occupied the area. So the operation succeeded in its purpose, even if the actual entrance to the tunnel was not definitely blocked. The railway was the object after all.

Jubilant at the dramatically devastating impact of these bombs, 617 Squadron looked forward to the chance of using them again. It came within a week. On 14 June – D+8 – Cheshire led a small section of Lancasters from 617 Squadron to attack the E-boat pens at Le Havre. The aim was to try and stop the activities of these vessels against the supply line of the Normandy beachhead. They carried Tallboy bombs to penetrate the thick concrete roofs designed to protect the pens from the air. The marker for the mission was once more Leonard Cheshire.

He was as determined as ever to leave an accurate mark for the following bombers, so he dived well below the altitude range of the anti-aircraft guns, which peppered the aircraft, the barrage gearing up to a great crescendo as he descended. They hit his aeroplane continually, but he still dived lower and lower, in daylight and with no cloud cover, only releasing his markers when he felt sure the devices would do their job. The aircraft was blazing, but somehow got out of that holocaust of Le Havre – and eventually to England again. The force following made several direct hits on the E-boat pens, and one of the Tallboy bombs pierced the roof, destroying part of the wall.

INDEX